Penguin Education

Penguin Education Specials
General Editor: Willem van der Eyken

State School
R. F. Mackenzie

State School
R. F. Mackenzie

Penguin Education

Penguin Education
A Division of Penguin Books Ltd,
Harmondsworth, Middlesex, England
Penguin Books Inc., 7110 Ambassador Road,
Baltimore, Md 21207, U.S.A.
Penguin Books Australia Ltd,
Ringwood, Victoria, Australia

First published 1970
Reprinted 1973
Copyright © R. F. Mackenzie, 1963, 1965, 1967, 1970
Parts of this text were originally published in
The Sins of the Children,
Escape from the Classroom
and *A Question of Living,*
all published by Collins

Made and printed in Great Britain by
C. Nicholls & Company Ltd
Set in Monotype Times

Contents

Author's Note

Braehead School, the subject of this book, is a mixed junior
secondary (secondary modern) school of 500 pupils in Buck-
haven, Fife, which opened in an old building in 1957 and is to be
shut down under the comprehensive organization in 1971. From
the three books published by Collins, *A Question of Living* (1963),
Escape from the Classroom (1965) and *The Sins of the Children*
(1967), I have selected extracts to present in a more concise form
what happens to a state school which experiments in education.
I am much indebted to Mr Edward Blishen, whose candid and
detailed criticism has made the presentation much more read-
able. And I'd like to express my gratitude to the Braehead staff, a
goodly company, now after all these years to be broken up.

Introduction

This book is about working-class children in the Scottish coalfield, and their fate in the post-war world. But it all began for me among middle-class children in Hampshire, before the war; and I must start my story there, since what I tried to put into practice in a state school in Fife in the fifties and sixties were some of the things I learned from the serene idealists of the Forest School, in the thirties.

The school was on the edge of a wood which sloped down to the Hampshire Avon, halfway between Salisbury and Bournemouth. Two large wooden buildings housed it. It was well-named: situated on the edge of the New Forest, it was surrounded by trees. The oakwoods and pines, in the middle of which the pupils lived, tinctured their lives. The two houses were a quarter of a mile apart and at night, going from one to the other through the wood, we learned to follow the line of the path by watching the break in the trees above, where the night sky and stars showed through. And the pupils measured the progress of the seasons by watching the changes in the woods.

For them the scarlet berries of spindle tree and butcher's broom, sparkling in the weakening sunlight of early autumn, compensated for the fading out of the summer. They jumped on puff balls to see the smoky powder expelled from their capsules, they collected mushrooms and felt a fearful delight in the treacherous mauves and verdigris greens and reds of death caps and the poisonous agarics. They crackled through the dry sticks brought down by the winds of late autumn sweeping through the beech woods and enjoyed the sound and feel of scuffling their shoes deep through the new layer of crisp dead leaves. They picked up fir cones which had been stripped of their seeds by hungry nuthatches.

It was in spring that the advantages of living in a wood came through most compulsively. Buds on the trees, daily becoming fatter, altered the trees' silhouettes against the milky sky; grass tips pushed through the biscuit coloured mat of last year's grass; and then wild geraniums, ground ivy, ivy-leaved toadflax crowded on one another.

I remember an athletic youngster of twelve who, after tea on a spring afternoon said, 'No, I won't be playing football tonight. I want to go round to the lab. I've some botany drawings to make.' Football, botany, they were equally parts of his love of living.

The pupils penetrated into the heathlands of the New Forest and brought back different kinds of heath. A bewildering richness of life that we hadn't known to exist was providing an enjoyment of colour and shapes. And I remember, too, an uninhibited girl pupil declaring, 'I love pleasure'. In those botany classes we were nearer, I think, to integrating education into a full enjoyment of life than I have usually been since. There was a full sensuous quality about it. There was drama in the discovery and the description of the deadly nightshade; and one bright, bright day out in the Forest in wet ground coming on a group of sundews and watching them absorb the insects they had trapped.

Forest School was run by a society called 'The Order of Woodcraft Chivalry'. Money had been left by a distinguished geologist and philosopher, Ernest Westlake, to buy two hundred acres of woodland and start a school that would put into practice the dreams of its founders. There hadn't been enough money to build stone school-houses, but wooden buildings did just as well. Westlake was a Quaker, and something of the Quaker serenity was in the educational philosophy on which the school was based.

It was an experiment, an effort to reshape education nearer to the heart's desire. 'Back to nature' was one of the principal themes, but there was also a concern with the latest psychological ideas. The background was a mixture of Red Indians and Freud. Easy now, looking back on it, to make fun of the whole business; and indeed there was a vein of rich comedy running through it. Many people made fun of it at the time. The founders weren't unduly disturbed. I think they had emotional reserves enough to know that people who confine their philosophizing to theoretical discussion are on safe ground, but that as soon as you try to put your own original ideas into practice the great gulf between the neatly-turned sentences in which they are enunciated and the raw and insufficient reality is bound to make you look silly. They were prepared to look silly, and go on.

The Order of Woodcraft Chivalry, discarding fossilized ritual but realizing that human beings need colour, had devised ritual of their own. For their meetings they wore strange druidical costumes. They re-baptized themselves with Red Indian names like Great Bear, Rising Sun, Laughing Water, Otter and Golden Eagle. In an effort to revive the realities of association in earlier times, the two big annual meetings of the society were given Saxon names. The summer meeting was called 'Folkmoot', the winter meeting 'Wassail'. When members met one another they raised their arms and uttered the greeting 'Blue Sky!' One Sunday every month there was a ritual meeting, outside if the weather was good, indoors if it was raining. The pupils wore their ceremonial uniforms, green shirts and trousers or skirts. The president said 'Let the Keeper of the Fire light the fire!' The Keeper stepped forward and there was silence as the glow spread into enveloping flames. Then the Keeper cried: 'Behold the fire! It leaps, it glows, it burns! So may the Great Spirit leap and glow and burn within you!'

The movement had much in common with the Scouts. Pupils were divided by age into groups called Elves, Woodlings, Trackers, Pathfinders. A much more charming description than our present terms: infants, primary, secondary. But unlike the Scout and Outward Bound movements, which have been content merely to add something to the existing educational system, the Order of Woodcraft Chivalry sought to alter profoundly the whole nature of education, within the classroom as well as outside. The training given in woodcraft was integrated with normal classroom work. Pupils were given tests when they were ready to move into a new group. These tests might include doing sums in long division: writing an essay on one of the Ransome books: swimming the Avon fully clothed and righting an upturned canoe. To get into the Tracker group you had to climb a specially difficult tree in the forest called the Tracker Tree. To enter an older group a pupil had to spend a night alone in the woods, beside a fire, and write an essay describing the experience and the thoughts that had come to him during his long, dark vigil.

The younger pupils didn't attend classroom lessons unless they wanted to. It worked. Sometimes a new pupil, transferred from an orthodox school, could hardly believe that he was really free to stay away from the classroom. He *would* stay away. The first week he would rove about the woods. The second week he would go to the kitchen and ask for jobs to do, getting coal, peeling potatoes, running errands. Then he began to be bored. He would go to the teacher and ask if he could go to a classroom, but only for one morning, and he'd seek assurance that his visit wouldn't be taken as a precedent. After that it was up to the teacher to make the lessons so interesting that the boy would wish to attend regularly.

One pupil I remember particularly who didn't go to lessons. His name was Pat. He had one consuming passion – radio. With the help of the music teacher, keen on amateur wireless, he spent his time making sets, improving reception. Coils and batteries littered his bed and bed-space, with blue-prints and books on wireless. Then one day the teacher said he couldn't teach him any more because further work would involve the relationships between EMF, current and resistance, and Pat couldn't work these things out because he couldn't do long multiplication and long division. Pat said: 'If I learn how to do them, will you tell me more about wireless?' The teacher said he would. Next morning Pat steamed off to the classroom and told the maths teacher his requirements. For a fortnight – morning, afternoon, and back again after tea – he spent long hours with more and more and longer sums, covering sheet after sheet of foolscap. Everybody he met he would ask: 'Give me a long division sum to do, a really hard one.' By the end of the fortnight he'd mastered these skills, and resumed his radio studies. In two weeks of concentrated study he had learned more than most pupils do in much longer periods.

There were very few rules. Pupils were forbidden to go on the main road, the roof or the river without permission. Hours of sleep were rigidly adhered to, and the children were very fit. I've sometimes wondered since how many of the troubles of children and adolescents (and indeed of adults) are due to insufficient sleep. For pupils over twelve, the school abandoned the theory that they should be free to attend lessons or not. It was pointed out to them that there were examinations to sit. Some of the questions were foolish, but they represented a hurdle anyone had to get over if he wanted to go further in his studies, or to the university. Most pupils accepted this situation philosophically enough. Most of them had already got so much out of the school that they could take a few hours of daily boredom in their stride. We never tried to tell them that boredom was good for them; only that we thought one day a more intelligent examination system would make it unnecessary.

In winter evenings when all the pupils were abed, the headmaster read books to us, such as James Stephens's *The Crock of Gold*. There's a luxury in being read to, even for adults. We sat there relaxed in body, and soon, our thoughts lazily following the images that the book called up, philosophers and leprechauns, and porridge with lumps in it, we were relaxed in mind too. It provided an ampler background against which to assess the busynesses of the workaday world. Following this excellent example, I spent all the time I had with senior pupils for a fortnight reading Axel Munthe's *Story of San Michele* aloud to them. I think it was the most lasting schoolwork I've done. Recently I met a pupil and it had remained in her memory as deeply as in mine. I described the attitude of listening to somebody reading aloud as relaxed but that doesn't adequately describe it. The pupils rushed to that lesson and said, 'Are we going to go on with *San Michele* today?' And in delight gave themselves to a mood of pure receptivity, sprawled about round the room. They let down their defences and felt involved right from the opening sentences, 'I sprang from the Sorrento sailing boat on to the little beach. Swarms of boys were playing among the upturned boats or bathing their shining bronze bodies in the surf, and the old fishermen in red Phrygian caps sat mending their nets outside the boathouses.' We could feel the Italian sun shining on the classical sculptures salvaged from the Tyrrhenian which Munthe had set up in his garden in Capri, we knew his neighbours. It was as if we were living at a depth not often reached in ordinary school work, as if we had penetrated a barrier into another dimension, as if we had a new freedom.

Once I was absent for a morning when a class was rehearsing the Falstaff scenes from *Henry IV* for a meeting of parents. I had said that the pupils would be able to continue the rehearsal unsupervised, but the headmaster looked in to see how things were going. The pupils shouted, 'Go away. We're busy'. He smiled and left them. Next day I got the impression that they were looking forward to the rehearsal with even more exuberance than usual, but how was I to know that during my absence they had laid aside the school editions of the play which we were using and had gone to the library to dig out the unexpurgated edition. They had obviously found what they were seeking and had already become word perfect. At that afternoon's rehearsal the speeches that greeted me, spoken with the utmost gusto, went like this:

Prince: I'll be no longer guilty of this sin; this sanguine coward, this bed presser, this horse-back breaker, this huge hill of flesh –

Falstaff: 'Sblood you starveling, you elf-skin, you dried neat's-tongue, you bull's pizzle, you stockfish! O! for breath to utter what is like thee; you tailor's yard, you sheath, you bow-case, you vile standing-tuck;

This broadside, delivered at top voice, drew hilarious mirth from the pupils.

The school was a clearing house of ideas on education and current affairs. A Jewish financial journalist who had left Germany, a film actor, a commercial artist, an industrialist would turn up on a Sunday afternoon and discuss things with the staff, or chat with the pupils while they bit their tea time sticks of celery. Not only the school doctor but the school psychiatrist made regular visits and would talk to the staff and discuss the theory and practice of experimental education. Local people would turn up in the evening. Down beside the river the Order had established a work camp for unemployed men, and these used often to share our plain suppers.

A Czech called Gustav, who had a small farm, looked in occasionally. Gustav was a tall, well-built man with the face and beard of a Hebrew prophet. I learned that he also had made an effort to rebuild society, having founded a group called 'The Harbingers of the Commonweal'. Gustav had a large innocence and an earnestness and wasn't making such a success of his farm, and perhaps his Commonweal if it had been brought to birth wouldn't have been much of a success either, like the Whiteway Colony. But I cannot help thinking that all this constructive phase in the thirties, however starry-eyed and idealistic and impractical and faintly ridiculous, was a valuable thing. And there were many such. We heard from time to time of the Woodcraft Folk (a separate group), the green-shirted Social Credit movement, and pacifists. One pacifist who sometimes came to the school and had spent a long time in prison, was in charge of reorganizing rural industries in three of the English counties. The chairman of his committee was a colonel. One day, he told me, the colonel accompanied him on a tour of the local industries that they had started or were supporting. It was a beautiful morning, the clouds drifted lazily over the Cotswolds, the smell of the hay was rich, and the honey-coloured Cotswold houses seemed incredibly perfect. 'What a wonderful land this is', the colonel said. 'And, do you know, some of these damned people, these pacifists, wouldn't fight for it.' Basil Robert said nothing. 'We had a day's work to do, and I didn't want to introduce an unharmonious note right at the beginning of it. Well, we did our day's work, visiting many rural industries, charcoal burning, metal work, ornamental gates, woodwork, and then at last when we were well on the way home in the evening I said, 'Colonel, you remember this morning referring to the pacifists who wouldn't fight for this beautiful country?'

'Yes', said the colonel, unthinkingly.

'Well, I was one of those pacifists.'

The colonel was silent for a few minutes. Then he turned and said, 'Robert, I'm sorry I spoke like that.'

Now out of this rural post war reconstruction in which warrior and pacifist were co-operating, in mutual respect, in the job of restoring country crafts, a historian might with reason have expected a new spirit of mutual understanding and goodwill. Living in Forest School and listening to the fecundity of ideas that were being propagated, he might have had further grounds for optimism. Goodwill, initiative, and the hard work in trying out ideas in practice seemed themselves to be excellent harbingers of a new commonweal.

We underestimated the difficulty; human life has less of the spirit of the Enlightenment and more of the spirit of the jungle than we supposed. Today the young, more realistic than we were, are looking for an alternative solution. In her book *On Violence* (1970) Miss Arendt says that the present glorification of violence is caused by severe frustration of the faculty of action, 'the ability to begin something new', in the modern world. Why is it that, thirty years later, the Forest School's vision of a common-weal is as far away as ever?

I think it's because politics cannot of itself achieve such a result; it is not even the main tool. Only now are reasons accumulating for saying that fundamentally this is a failure of education. If you are going to create a new society, it is in the schools that you must begin. But education has remained a creaking, ramshackle construction – like an old windmill that goes on flapping its great arms long after the miller has left. Its purpose has been so to indoctrinate the majority that they would give as little trouble as possible to the minority in power. There is repairing and patching of this system, toiling over irrelevant things. At a meeting to discuss the introduction of comprehensive education, the secondary headmasters of Fife spent nearly three hours talking about how much of the eleven plus could be retained temporarily during the change-over period. In Edinburgh, Scottish teachers, many of them able, spend countless hours discussing details of questions in past external examination papers. They are fiddling while Rome burns. Incest increases, children play with drugs, school-girls have babies, there is increasing violence, but the earnest educators go on discussing the scaling of marks, details of verbal reasoning tests, pools of ability, the wording of questions in examinations – a wearying and unrewarding labour of Sisyphus.

A future generation will, I believe, regard this absorption as incredulously as we now regard the medieval discussions of how many angels could dance on the point of a pin. It points to something that I think has been insufficiently understood; the power of educational indoctrination. We can be so educated that we can spend some of the best years of our lives engaged in completely valueless endeavours; and, except at rare moments, we can remain unaware that we are doing so. The pupils of Britain are being brainwashed; and their teachers, a product of the same process, perpetuate the operation.

The initiatives of that experimental period in English education, in the twenties and thirties when the Forest School flourished, were not followed up. We thought that dawn would broaden into boundless day. For some of us, A. S. Neill was the prophet of a new age. All his books were at hand, in a bookcase in the staffroom. Not that the staff of Forest School were agreed about Neill's ideas. He brought into the school not peace but a sword. We were a Menshevik school, and Neill was the uncompromising Bolshevik, the extremist. All sorts of weird tales percolated through to Hampshire from the educational frontier in Suffolk, where Neill was running his pioneer school, Summerhill. The more I read of Neill's books myself, the more did he seem to me to have the rights of it. But there were fierce staff meetings – discussions when the disciplines of the old order threatened to creep back.

Now most of the bright promise of those progressive schools, contrary to our expectations, have been submerged under the forces of the establishment. Almost alone, Neill stands out, a stubborn pillar in the rising tide. By various compromises, the other pioneer schools have made their peace. At the same time, the more innocuous advances have been incorporated into a large number of state schools. These early educational experiments have a permeating effect, and will continue to have it; yet I would say that the establishment has won. Its triumph will be short-lived. The price of victory will be paid with the violence of the nineteen-seventies.

My bed-sitting room at Forest School was a little wooden hut. One day I found that a pupil had made pencil drawings on the wall. I guessed who it was and asked her if she had made the drawings. She said she had. Angrily I told her to wipe them off. My room was also used by a visiting teacher of Spanish, and after one of his lessons he said: 'Who is the artist?'

I said: 'Which artist?'

'The one who's made these excellent drawings on the walls of your hut.'

Rather shamefacedly I told him. He said: 'She has real talent.'

After he'd gone, I went to look at them. I hadn't thought to look at them, really to look at them, before. I had been brought up in the tradition that you don't draw on walls. Walls are there to be kept clean. They were good drawings, right enough, and I felt honoured to have them decorating my room. But that evening when I returned from schoolwork they were gone. I hadn't thought to tell the pupil that there was now a new outlook on wall drawings. She had come in with a scrubbing brush and removed them.

That was a lesson I never forgot – one of those learned at the Forest School that I tried to apply when, twenty years later, I found myself in a harsher set-up altogether.

Chapter One
The School

This is the story of what one state school made of the attempt to alter the age-old and admired national system of education.

Those who ran the school were up against many difficulties. It is a junior secondary school (or secondary modern, as the English equivalent is called); and the pupils, three-quarters of the population of the Coal Town, are those who have not been offered the opportunity of entering the high school for senior secondary education. Most (but not all) of the parents who are interested in their children's education feel that these youngsters have been marked as failures, since for these parents education means the traditional Scottish academic education. They feel the work we do in the school isn't really education at all, and they have misgivings about us, and are pre-disposed to be critical.

I can understand how they feel. For twelve years they have been watching the miracle of a child's growth, eager to note signs of a good intelligence, proudly laying up the child's sayings in their hearts. And saving money against the day when a son or daughter would go to the university. And then, when the child was twelve, there was the sudden shock, the shattering of high hopes, the end to day-dreams.

A father came one day to talk about his boy. He spoke quietly, resigned. 'We always thought, his mother and I, that he was a bright laddie. I have a shed and in my spare time I do a lot of carpentry. He used to come in and help me, and then he started making things himself. He made a bookcase, and he bought a blue-print and rigged up a wireless set for himself. Pretty good reception, too. We bought encylopedias from a traveller that came to the house and we encouraged him to read them; and he did. He used to spend a lot of time in winter evenings, reading about science.' The father stopped, and then after a pause added, almost apologetically, 'Oh well. Maybe we built up our hopes too high.' He smiled, a slight, sad smile. 'Ye always think your ain bairns are pretty good. Better than they really are, I suppose.'

There is something seriously wrong with an educational system that ruthlessly destroys a parent's hopes for a child when he is eleven or twelve, and as a consequence (for the child senses his parents' disappointment in him) decreases the child's confidence in himself.

Parents who have watched the miracle of birth and growth are briefly informed that the miracle is over. Their children are just ordinary. The magic has fled and the wonder gone out of life. This is one of the saddest things of our time, and its consequences are difficult to calculate. At the age of twelve, hope is given up for three-quarters of the children in the country. They are regarded by their parents, and by themselves, as have-beens.

The attitude of many of us teachers towards children has been subtly infected by our knowledge of the measurement that has been made of their intelligence, through intelligence tests.

One day I was thumbing through some reports and my eye alighted on the intelligence quotient of a pupil of mine. To me he had always seemed a bright, energetic boy, full of mischief and happiness. But now a cloud dimmed that brightness and I thought, 'What a pity!' And I realized that the boy had been diminished in my eyes. Next time I saw him I'd think not of a cheerful boy but of a disappointingly low intelligence quotient, and be condescendingly sympathetic towards him.

This is the prevailing climate in education. I have heard a woman teacher, normally kind and intelligent, refer to her class of girls of slightly under-average intelligence as 'just dross'. She was not angrily expressing an emotion about a class which had been giving trouble. She was, she imagined, expressing a scientific fact, based on a psychological measure of their intelligence. And it is my criticism of the present educational departments that, in spite of their fine words about a fair deal for the 'intellectually under-privileged', they share the outlook expressed by their teacher with such blunt honesty. Pupils, in the prevailing educational opinion, are primarily intellects to be trained. For efficient training they have to be sorted out into groups of like intellectual capacity. Philosophers throughout the ages have debated what the word 'good' means, but the educationists have no doubts. The good pupil is the pupil with high intelligence.

Psychologists, I know, are reasonable, humane people, aware

of the clumsiness and inaccuracy of their measuring instruments. But their occupational trouble is that they themselves cannot help being taken in by the seeming accuracy of intelligence quotients. IQ 79, not 78 or 80. It gives the psychologist the feeling that he has John Jones taped. But it is not so. I am not religious and do not belong to any church but, between the psychologist who thinks of John Jones as 'IQ 79' and the religious man who thinks of him as 'a child of God', I am wholeheartedly on the side of the religious man because his description, for all the pathetic inadequacy of language to sum up a human being, is at least an effort to put into words the infinite possibilities of John Jones.

In order to give the pupils practice in the working of democracy, the school has a council instead of a prefect system. Candidates, proposed and seconded, make a brief appearance on the platform at the school assembly. The pupils vote in the same way as their elders do at a parliamentary election, and the sixteen successful candidates form the council for the year. They meet once a week and discuss damage done to a bicycle, theft of money from another pupil, Friday evening dances, raising £15 for an invalid girl in Athens sponsored by the Save the Children Fund, the introduction of rules for the stairs so that a little girl, walking upstairs, won't be knocked over by a big boy racing down. The girls suggested that mirrors should be put up in the new lavatories, and the authorities agreed.

Sometimes they have to make contact with the Town Council. The School Council supported whole-heartedly a suggestion made by a teacher that they should get spades and shovels and excavate the silted-up open-air swimming pool on the beach, and they asked the Town Council's permission. From time to time a pupil asked at meetings of the School Council what further progress had been made. The Town Council delayed their reply because of sewage difficulties, and because they thought the plan was not very practicable. When the pupils were critical of the Town Council I reminded them of certain work they had themselves undertaken and not followed up. They began to be ruefully tolerant of the Town Councillors, realizing what a gulf lies between the enthusiastic support of a proposal (such as that the pupils should take a major part in running their Friday evening dances) and the working out of the details (a relay of pupils taking money at the door, the safe depositing of the money, seeing that the gramophone records are available, seeing that throughout the evening somebody is responsible for the records so that none are stolen, arranging for the lemonade and sweets to be on sale from the school shop, clearing up afterwards). I think the School Council has learned that democracy means more than the first heady passing of a resolution and the later criticism of *them* for not speedily putting it into effect.

This experiment in self-government could hardly be called successful. The Council have had considerable success in recovering stolen property and money. Because nobody is punished for stealing and because the Council deals with it, pupils who would not dream of telling teachers about seeing money stolen, have no hesitation in informing Council members. The Council recovers the stolen goods, and, since these meetings are conducted privately, the staff do not generally know who is responsible for the theft. But in other ways the Council have been less successful. I had hoped that by now they would be arranging their own meetings, preparing the agenda, discussing quietly, and carrying out their own decisions; but it doesn't work like that so far. Yet I feel that this is a more valuable way of getting pupils to take an understanding and active part in running their own country than giving them a history of Parliament. In the School Council they are dealing with issues that are real to them – the persistent offenders, for example – and they realize that to many questions there are no 'correct answers' as there are to questions in arithmetic. They realize, too, that their own attempts to provide answers, although different from an adult's, are worth trying out and may sometimes be proved more successful than those which are usually accepted.

It is not easy to be a good Council member. Some pupils, with wonderful independence, give a judgement against members of their own gang or group, and suffer for it in loss of popularity. They don't complain about this. But they do complain when impatient teachers tell them in class that they are supposed, as Council members, to show an example and that they are failing to do so.

A journalist was associated with the school for a year. Every time he thought we were heading for a quiet backwater he kept pushing the school and its pupils back into the main stream. 'How about getting the pupils on to some of the Z cars?' he said one day, and, although he wasn't as successful as that, he got the ready co-operation of the police in showing the pupils the real background to the activity of the police patrol cars. Another time he came to suggest that he should take a group – perhaps the group that was producing the school's weekly newspaper – to see the Court of Session and the Court of Criminal Appeal in Edinburgh, and, after that, to visit an Edinburgh newspaper.

I was impressed by the story the pupils brought back from these encounters and wrote for their own paper. An advocate who had appeared for the crown in several capital murder trials took them round. They saw the Judges, these pillars of society, as ordinary human beings, talking in the great Parliamentary Hall without their robes. Then they saw them with their robes and the pupils were surprised at the difference this made, the meta-morphosis of an ordinary human being into the majesty of *the law*. The advocate took them to watch a case in which some men were appealing against convictions of whisky stealing. The advo-cate set off with the pupils on a tour and discussion of the processes of the law. Perhaps it was something in the bearing of our pupils, naïve and bewildered, which caught his interest. Perhaps he felt that they were 'the people', the citizens in whose name and for whose protection the whole resplendent edifice of the judiciary is built and for no other reason; and that they should now be informed at first hand what the lawyers were doing in their name. I don't know. But from what the teachers told me about the afternoon's visit, I gathered that he spoke and acted as if he regarded himself as proud to be a servant of the public and that he showed an uncondescending respect for the pupils, treating them gravely, as his equals, and considering their opinions as worthy of careful consideration. The pupils saw several prisoners handcuffed together. A fourteen-year-old girl was aghast. It was the men who had lost their appeal in the whisky-stealing case and they were being taken to a prison van. The advocate treated with respect the children's honest and honestly-spoken criticism. They asked what crown counsel does.

'He merely states the case against the accused. The Crown doesn't put people in prison. It is the jury that does that. You may feel that there are things wrong with the law. When you grow up, it will be up to you to alter the law.'

This, I felt, was living education. In the school's badge is a fish, and its bones and organs are shown. The reason is to indicate not only the fishing background of the Coal Town, but that the pupils are encouraged to inquire below the superficial appearance of things to find the truth. This is what the advocate had done for the pupils. He had shown them the men within the robes, the harsh reality of the cells and the handcuffs outside the grandeur of the Appeal Court, and the possibility that one day the pupils would carefully consider their laws and amend their faults. The establishment became for one afternoon not a remote, impersonal and therefore vaguely hostile institution, but a living institution which is run by human beings and therefore capable of faults and which our pupils could take a hand in and improve. The gulf had been bridged for a day. The advocate had regarded the pupils as, like himself, parts of the institution. My own instinct is all against the establishment, and I feel that the only way to deal with it is to fight it. But it is possible that a less wearing, less friction-causing and ultimately more valuable way is to join it, become part of it, and alter it from within. This is what the advocate, probably all unaware, was indicating.

It was a refreshing change from the usual school attitudes where pupils memorize neatly packaged opinions, are preached at about their duties and their sins, and brought up to be efficient servants of a society run for an object beyond their understanding and participation. Perhaps the future of the world depends on which of these educational attitudes emerges – willing co-operation and involvement, or suspicious and drilled conscription of people for the machine.

I once thought of education as a commodity in the market; a commodity for which teachers had to create the demand. But we don't have to create the demand; we don't need high-pressure salesmanship designed to sell the public something they don't really need. The need for education is already there, as claimant as the need for food. 'Why?' asks the child. 'Why? Why? Why did that herd of red deer come down this corrie and not that one? Why is that green rock in the bay so slippery? Why are these anemones so bright blue and those in my grandfather's garden so pale blue? Why do these seashells have such funny shapes, like the tops of ice-cream cones? Why are lobsters' gills poisonous to eat? Why do soft things like ferns leave fossil markings beneath millions of tons of rock?' There are few teachers who are willing to sacrifice quantity of information in order to follow the gleam of a child's real interests. But there are some. The Coal Town school is lucky in having more than its share of them. One was a doctor of science, a distinguished research worker with a wide cultural background and deep human sympathies who brought to teaching all the searching intelligence and the attitude of no-questions-barred that he had brought to scientific research. He found, in dealing with his pupils, a demand on all his abilities, intellectual and sympathetic, a call on all his power of understanding, that he hadn't found elsewhere. One day while he was, like an orthodox teacher, following the scheme of work which gave one lesson to filing and melting glass tubing, he discovered that his pupils had suddenly become absorbed in what they were doing – melting glass, pulling it out like chewing-gum, experimenting happily in making shapes. Instead of stopping them and saying, 'Now, let's be finished with play and get on with science,' he suddenly realized that *this was science*. The children were absorbed with the plasticity of melted glass; they were conducting their own inquiries into the nature of things. This was science, the teacher said, because there was in it the delight of the artist and the curiosity of the child. And it seemed to me significant that when I mentioned this incident to an art teacher, he, too, decided to give his pupils the opportunity to mould shapes out of melted glass tubing, providing them with a new medium in which to give reality to their dreams and imaginings.

In our schools we don't do nearly enough of this. We banish pleasure of this kind from our classrooms. This is a pity, because a pupil's first interest in things arises from this kind of sensuous observation. Young children like to stroke furs and feel the soft touch of feathers, to let a spoonful of syrup trickle back into a mound in a jar and to watch the mound lose its shape in the smooth shining top of the surface of the syrup in the jar. They can spend a long time letting fine, dry sand run through their fingers and, like the syrup, lose itself in the sand it is running into. They watch raindrops racing uncertainly down windows, and they are fascinated by the sight of drops of mercury coalescing. Amazing stuff, mercury. A liquid, but not wet like a liquid. And unexpectedly heavy. I once watched a boy of twelve, a farmer's son, playing with blobs of mercury. There were one big blob and several tiny ones, and he was, with a tiny stick, gently propelling a tiny blob along towards the big one. Then, all of a sudden, the tiny blob would disappear in the substance of the big one; yet the big blob kept its spherical shape. Then the boy brought up the next tiny blob, and finally he got them all united within the substance of the big one. 'It's just like a hen taking all her chickens under her for safety,' he said.

Similarly children are amused for a long time watching small balls rolling down a smooth slope, and balloons floating in the air, and mud squeezing through their fingers, and methylated spirits drying on their hands, and motes dancing in the sunbeams. A visitor to the school pointed to a small boy who was mixing colours and daubing them on a white paper. 'All the time I've been here,' she said, 'he hasn't done anything but play with his paints. He hasn't tried to paint a picture. He's wasting his time.' The teacher gave the visitor a sermon on the subject of what it really means to waste time, pointing out that the pupil was experimenting with colours and enjoying it. He argued that it is no small thing for a pupil to find happiness in so simple a pleasure as mixing colours. But that if earnest people demand further results from an hour spent by a child with a paintbox and a brush, it is as well to remember that when the child has exhausted his interest in putting daubs of paint on paper he will try out something else, and that the teacher's job is to watch the widening scope and encourage it, until it expands into a picture.

Pictures painted in just such a way by the Coal Town pupils were requested for an exhibition of their own held for a fortnight in Dundee, and then in Aberdeen for six weeks. Similarly, from an absorbed interest in mercury and raindrops and sand, pupils have investigated the phenomena of 'this braw, bricht, birlin' earth', which seem merely dull when we give them scientific

names like surface tension and fusion and friction and accelera-
tion and ask the pupils to learn the definitions of these things.

Here, I think, I'm fairly near the heart of the matter. One of
the serious ailments of education is due to the banishing of the
senses from education. A child's first visit to a rock pool is a vivid
sensuous experience. He watches the flickering sun-beams strike
the bottom of the pool, and the swimming of the transparent
and almost invisible prawns and the walking about of the peri-
winkles, as unexpected as it would be to see marbles sticking out
feet and walking. He enjoys the colour of the anemones, and
fearfully and compulsively puts his fingers against their pro-
truding tentacles to feel what will happen. But these things do
not much enter into a biology teacher's scheme of things. Instead,
the pupil must memorize classifications and deal with animals
under the headings of contractility, irritability, digestion, excre-
tion and reproduction. It is amazing how dull even a subject like
biology can become in the hands of teachers trained to work
hard and, as the saying is, 'get results'. Verily, verily, they have
their reward.

The art department is one of the pivots round which the school
revolves. For the art staff, art is not a 'subject' but a way of life.
It is the cultivation of a love of excellence, and it doesn't matter
whether the excellence, the distinction, is shown in a picture or
a dance or simply in an action in everyday life. Under the skilful
but unobtrusive guidance of the art teachers, pupils find the
world a brighter place than they had imagined, and gradually
they wake up to its possibilities. Roaming along the shore, they
keep an eye open for the shapes of the pieces of rock that lie
there, and they pick up and bring back to the school suitable
pieces of sandstone which they feel could be fashioned easily into
the likeness of a terrier's head or a human face. It was at the
shore that they found red clay, brought it into the school in
buckets and made likenesses of one another and of people whom
they had seen on television. It is a curious thing, this desire to
create and to find a peg, any peg, on which to hang their creations.
One morning our pupils, seeking for something further to model
in red clay, adopted the theme of 'refugees'. It was World
Refugee Year and schools had been asked to tell their pupils

about it. An art teacher said to his class, 'What is the first thing you think about when I mention refugees?'

Some pupils replied, not surprisingly, 'They're always hungry.'

The teacher said, 'What happens if you're always hungry?'

'You become thin,' said one pupil.

'Your bones show through,' said another.

'This morning,' said the teacher, 'I have a human skull for you to examine so that you will understand the bone structure of the face. Then you will go to the beach for more red clay, and see if you can make a figure which shows what you feel it is like to be a refugee.'

From then on the teacher's role was in the background. He put a large mat near the door so that the pupils wouldn't carry clay from the studio floor through the rest of the school.

An unexpected richness and imagination showed through the pupils' work. There was a figure of an old man with empty eyes, forgetting the refugee camp while he played on a melodeon the tunes of his native land.

One pupil, who said that the first thing she thought of was that refugees have no possessions, made a figure of a mother fiercely holding on to her only possession – a child. There was the gaunt head of a beautiful girl, an arresting Epstein-like work. Humanity was penetrating into the school from the trouble-centres of the world, through art, more intensively and more memorably than any other way.

'Is it not strange that sheep's guts should hale souls out of men's bodies?' says Benedick in *Much Ado about Nothing*. I felt the same about the red clay from the Coal Town's shore.

Help is given to any pupils who wish to convert an idea into a reality. Two boys went to one of the art teachers and said they wanted to make a puppet theatre. Perhaps they had seen something of the sort in a television programme. The teacher said, 'All right; go ahead.'

'We need wood. Where will we get wood?'

'I'm afraid the County Council won't provide you with wood to make a puppet theatre. You'll have to find your own.'

'But where?'

'That's up to you.'

They searched the beach and returned with several pieces.

They asked the teacher how to make the theatre. He said, 'Look; you just go ahead and make it. You can find out as you go along.' They nailed the wood together and sat down to think what they could do to make their four-sided proscenium rigid. It sometimes swivelled and changed shape when pressure was put upon it. Then they re-discovered one of the major human discoveries – that a triangle is rigid; and that, by making a cross-piece, they could transform their wobbly rectangular stage into a rigid one. After that, they set about making their own puppets, with the art teacher's help. From the pleasure of seeing papier-mâché figures growing under their hands and assuming changed appearances from random touches with a paint brush, they went on to explore more fully this possibility of giving apparent life to puppets. This opened up a whole realm. The pupils were ready to put into puppet-play any activity that came within their ken. Pupils like to play, and, as a headmaster of mine once pointed out, that is all that a play is – merely play. The young child says, 'We'll play at railways; I'll be the engine'; and he goes chuck-chuck-chuck round the garden. Older pupils play at being their parents and teachers (and, in so doing, reveal to us, without malice, the kind of people that their parents and we, their teachers, are, as they see us). Adults play at being Shylock.

The trouble is that you can't do something as simple as 'playing' in a school without the educationists fetching up alongside and boarding you and saying, 'Play, eh? Now we'll organize this for you. You might be doing something about the history of the *drama*. The pupils should learn to appreciate perhaps a little scene from Aristophanes – *The Frogs*, for example. Some Shakespeare. And then you might go on to Bridie. Of course you want to do it properly. Mustn't be too easy. Got to think of your best pupils, you know. Something to stretch them. So we'll give you an examination. Here's a specimen paper. As you can see, there are questions on Shakespeare's comic characters. Bottom, perhaps; and Falstaff . . . .' And so on it goes, breaking your heart if you take it seriously. Because you know that when the formal educationists come in at the door, education escapes through the window. On one hand there is Maureen Smith of the Coal Town, who can make you split your sides with laughter as she plays the part of her aunt at Sunday afternoon tea; on the other hand there are the educationists, who want to examine Maureen's ability to write the correct things about Shylock as a tragic character in a comedy, in order that Maureen's prospective employers can know how many marks Maureen made in 'English'. (But not all employers are impressed by certificates and marks.)

Some parents, also, complain that there is too much 'play' in the school. Life should be, as a Scottish character said, 'a wrastle wi' the Deil'. The Puritan tradition persists. There is something wrong if the pupils are enjoying themselves, playing. But they are not enjoying themselves if they are learning speeches about the quality of mercy or the evil that men do, or writing answers to questions about Macbeth's witches. Therefore that kind of play is beyond reproach.

Thus even in a small community like the Coal Town school, it is difficult to let pupils 'play' unless you can dress up their play in high-sounding terms to make it seem as dull as the treaties in a history book. And timetabling is difficult. Here they are, all set to make a play, about characters either in the Coal Town or in the greater world reported in the newspapers and the television news programmes. They could spend many fruitful hours trying out scenes, modifying, scrapping, remaking, unaware of time. But the period bells ring, and, creators absorbed in their creation, they throw down their tools angrily, and stalk off to the next subject on the timetable. How does a school make a compromise between the demands of pupils absorbed in making a puppet play and the demands of a timetable?

On good days the pupils go down to the old sea town and sketch the fishermen's old houses, due for demolition, and later make full-size pictures of them. They sit high up against the art-room window and make pictures of the street below, having learned that the street surface is not a black tarred monochrome as they had thought, but is full of colour; they look at the colours and try to put them on paper. Pupils who have been hearing about the story of the earth try to put on paper what they imagine a swampy carboniferous forest (in the underground darkness of which their parents work, under the school and under the Forth) was like when it flourished on the earth's surface. Prehistoric animals fascinate them. Dinosaurs rampage across their pictures. One Christmas it was decided to use the motif of the prehistoric world for the decorations of the hall for the school parties, and for a fortnight all the art rooms were turned over to painting pictures. At the end of that time steamy jungles, horrific reptiles and swarming life proliferated over the walls. One parent came to complain that for a fortnight her son had done no work in the school. I found that for the whole fortnight her boy had been in an art room turning out pictures and reading encyclopedias and illustrated books. While he was finding out what an archaeopteryx was like, his imagination would be kindled by a score of other things – the wingless waterfowl hesperornis, the flying ichthyornis, the rhinoceros-like triceratops, and primeval vegetation like magnolias and the plumed sigillaria trees. He took some books home and thumbed them over in the evenings. All this I told his mother. 'I knew that,' she said. 'He's been taking encyclopedias home and reading them to all hours. But he hasn't been doing any of the usual school work. I mean the kind of work that will help him to be transferred from here to the High School!'

Another Christmas the theme of the decorations was the past of the Coal Town. The school hall was covered by murals of what the pupils, judging from the old houses along the shore, imagined the eighteenth-century town had been like. When a great fire was burning on the wide hearth and the doors were shut, we felt we were in an eighteenth-century square as friendly and cosy as a picture from Hans Andersen's tales. Fish-nets, lobster pots and figures of many kinds of fish hung from the ceiling, and a gigantic figure of Neptune, thirty feet high, bestrode the fireplace, regarding the scene. A cheerless building had been transfigured, and in these surroundings the Christmas parties were held. On the last day of the term, when the festivities were over, the janitor asked what was to be done about the figure of Neptune, and the staff said the only thing to do was to burn it. At dinner-time a large party of pupils and staff took the figure to the shore. The conflagration started in the atmosphere of elation which any blaze causes, but gradually a sadness took over, as if the pupils were watching a funeral pyre. We hadn't realized how affectionate they'd grown towards the giant, a familiar figure who had become part of the school, the presiding genius of the hearth. One pupil said to a teacher, 'We should have made a raft and fixed Neptune on the raft and set fire to it and pushed it out into the Forth and watched it go out with the tide and disappear in the distance.'

The story of human reproduction was what most readily caught the interest of the pupils. I find it difficult to understand the fuss that is made about telling pupils how babies are born. The pupils are so entranced by this story that there is no difficulty in teaching them. Once I had a mixed class and said that I was thinking of telling them about reproduction, but if some of them felt they would be embarrassed I wouldn't go on with it. I asked them to write anonymously on a piece of paper whether they wished to have the class or not. Everybody wrote 'Yes' except two pupils; one girl who wrote 'No' and then scored it out and wrote 'Yes', and a boy who wrote 'Yes, yes, yes'. The pupils weren't embarrassed; they were too interested to be embarrassed, and they asked questions freely.

A school doctor told me another school had asked him to give a talk (only one talk) to senior boys on sex, and he was going to give to it the greatest possible preparation and care. To him it was an ordeal. I think pupils must find adults extremely difficult to understand.

A private firm, which manufactures sanitary goods for women, sends round a woman doctor to lecture to schoolgirls on female hygiene. She does no advertising of the firm's goods, apart from sending, after her visits, instructional films in the introduction to which the firm's name is mentioned. First she gave to the older girls a simple talk on female physiology, dealing mostly with menstruation. I asked her why the talk was limited to the older girls, since medical statistics indicated that menstruation was beginning at an earlier age. She told me that menstruation now in fact began for a considerable number of girls in the primary school. (It would be interesting to know how many primary schools in Britain have made provision for this). Since an Education Department science inspector had said that girls of the first year of the secondary school (that is, girls of twelve) should be taught the physiology of reproduction, I asked her to lecture also to these. Later she told me that, although the girls had listened attentively to the lecture, they had been too embarrassed to ask the questions they would clearly have liked to ask. In another school, she said, the senior girls had been invited to write questions anonymously and put them in envelopes, and she had answered the questions as she opened the envelopes before the whole group of girls.

It was agreed that this method would be tried out in the Coal Town School. After some initial doubts, the girls wrote out many questions, and the lecturer courageously answered them all, except one which dealt with a refinement of sex play.

The questions were illuminating. They showed that these girls of fourteen varied from the very sophisticated who had had sexual experience, to the very innocent. There were questions about the Coal Town vocabulary of sex, fear deriving from old wives' tales about menstruation, conflict between the desire to be naughty and the desire to be nice at the same time. There was inquiry about the male reproductive organs. There were naïve questions about whether there was a male equivalent of menstruation, and whether you should let a boy kiss you when you had your periods; and a question about what to do and where to get more information from a girl whose periods had not begun, who said her mother never spoke to her about these things and that she was scared her periods might begin when she was alone in the house.

It was a picture of an adventurous, frightened, uninstructed, bewildered group of children, hungry for authentic information and guidance. They are scared at the vehemence of their own desires, shame-faced at their own questions about sex, and unable to make some sort of accord between the way they feel and the way that their elders seem to assume they ought to act. This is a vital question of our time, more vital than our technical competence to survive in a world of moon rockets. What do we tell our children about sex? Exactly what answer do we give to the girl who asked what she should do when she felt like submitting to her boy-friend's advances?

On Monday nights forty to sixty pupils turned up in the technical department of our school in the Coal Town to build boats, several girls among them. For two years there was no grant from public funds or school money to buy wood for this voluntary work, and the pupils collected silver paper and scrap metal and

made and sold toffee to raise money. Two members of the technical department helped them, unpaid, on these Monday evenings.

One February morning I went to watch the launching of three
pupil-built canoes and of an old skiff presented to the school and
repaired in the woodwork shop. Round the harbour were derelict
buildings, a blocked-up ruin where the blacksmith used to work,
a deserted scene where once the fishermen gathered round the
big barometer, their hands deep in their front-placed trouser-
pockets, listening to the chapping of the smith's hammer on the
anvil. Pieces of old iron lay around, black mud, horse-dung and
tin cans, chocolate boxes, cigarette packets and onion peelings.
The harbour is now separated from the sea by a large bank of
coal refuse, and only the highest of tides splash over the bank
and bring sea-water into it. The water of the harbour is usually
stagnant. Rubbish is thrown into it, pieces of wire, stones and
old bedsteads. Along the black bank separating it from the sea,
horses and carts, carrying sea-coal picked up on the shore, have
made a black muddy track, and the track goes right over the old
west wall of the harbour. The old lifeboat station (roofless but
strong-walled) is cut off from the sea by black earth from the pit
bing, deposited by waves during the last twenty-five years. Two
or three hundred yards away, over a level extent of pit refuse, lies
the former swimming-bath, now entirely dry and silted up. The
eroding red sandstone strata enclose the bay, at an angle to the
horizontal, sticking out of the grassy slopes.

I had asked the Town Council for permission to use the old
harbour. The Town Clerk said it did not belong to the Council.
Nobody was sure whom it belonged to, but it was probably
owned jointly by the fishermen who had built it for the safe
anchorage of their boats. But now that most of the fishermen
were gone, nobody was likely to dispute the school's using the
harbour to launch canoes in. But the Town Clerk pointed out
that the town had been having a lot of trouble because the tides,
having washed away the pit refuse from the bing, were washing
it up once more against the outfall of the sewers, clogging them,
and it was possible that the contents of one of the sewers were
seeping through into the stagnant water of the harbour.

Nevertheless, we decided to go ahead with the launching of the
canoes. That morning I was delayed (discussing with the Youth

Employment Officer the chances that one of our girls would have of getting a job in a garage after completing a technical course in motor engineering) and I walked down to the harbour some time after the others. When I rounded the corner all the boats were in the water, and being paddled around, and thirty pupils stood round the wooden jetty, made in the school. It's a scene I shall remember for a long time. The February sun was shining on the smooth water of the harbour and the pupils were thoroughly enjoying themselves; not only because of this un-expected opportunity for the release of energy, but also because they were trying themselves out against a new medium, in boats made by their own hands. It was like a surge of new, eager life in a dead place. The old fishermen would have been happy to see it. And maybe the pupils themselves, sons of coal miners though they are, felt vaguely some awareness that they had roots in the sea, and that their grandfathers and great-grandfathers had lived on it and forced a living out of it.

On the north-east coast of the county, where the Tay estuary broadens into the North Sea, new land is being deposited faster than anywhere else in Britain by the action of sea currents. Parties of our school pupils have been taken in the school bus to work here, unpaid, and, during breaks in their work, to study the area. Here even geological changes have been speeded up. No one is sure why. Away inland, in the centre of Scotland, in a region drained by the tributaries of the Tay, bulldozers have been tearing the soil about, so that tunnels and dams can be built for the hydro-electric development, and it is possible that more and more soil has been carried past Dundee and dropped where the Tay meets contrary sea-currents. And the off-shore winds may have something to do with it. Previously they blew back the waves that carried gravel, but now the Forestry Commission's pine-woods protect the coastal strip from the off-shore winds, and the waves deposit their gravel and sand uninterrupted. Between the 1940 line of cement blocks, put down to prevent enemy landings, and the sea, there is now a quarter of a mile of new land. Here many sorts of plants have arrived to colonize the virgin soil and the Nature Conservancy is studying them, to find what plants estab-lish themselves under natural conditions. The experiment is complicated by thousands of seedling fir-trees which owe their origin to the Forestry Commission's wood, that is, to artificial conditions; and our pupils had to uproot the fir-trees in the new territory. But they studied also the plants and the birds which are colonizing the new land, and helped the students of St Andrews University when they made their annual measurement of the new land. In this same region, but farther inland, they made paths to the bird-hides at the edge of a loch, and planted willows and firs to hide these approaches from the water-fowl on the lochs, and, in their spare time, watched from the hides the coots, widgeon and eider-ducks swimming in the loch. And they were complimented by the Nature Conservancy for the energetic and valuable work they did.

I expected the pupils would work well, but the vigour and drive of the enterprise exceeded our hopes.

The whole business seemed symbolic. These pupils need a completely fresh start. I hadn't realized, before, the extent to which the education committees of Britain, the conveners, the directors, the inspectors, the professors, had lost touch with this suspicious, potentially generous but uncommitted new generation. I hadn't realized the gulf between these pupils, so responsive to even the smallest efforts to meet their needs, and their elders, conscientious, sincere but unimaginative, and unaware that the education system has no nourishment to offer. It is difficult to show to these education committee members the energy and goodwill that their broken-down educational system is neglecting, and the achievements that are immediately possible if they would only wake up to the situation. The only way I can describe it is to compare it to a turmoil of waters churning round angrily above a dam, which, when released, flows with a shining quiet beauty. It is so easy to lift the sluice and let this power go free, and so rewarding. The school's main purpose is to lift the sluice, so that this power can be used.

One May morning we invited a Fife minister of the Church of Scotland, who was chairman of the BBC's 'Nature Scrapbook' programmes, to take a group of our pupils, who were camping, through a Fife wood. With his help the pupils found the nests of a hedge-sparrow, thrush, wood pigeon, blackbird and kestrel.

One pupil said that the kestrel's nest, storey upon storey, looked like a boarding-house. In a trap they found a stoat, and later a partridge. They caught two leverets and then freed them. They found two pheasants' eggs, cooked, in a tinker's roadside fire. There had probably been a dozen, said the minister, and the tinkers had had a good meal and these left were the only two that the tinkers had lost among the ashes. They listened to the willow-warbler and the wren and the quieter song of the robin ('a wee trickle of notes').They found a dead mouse in a tree-nest where a hawk may have dropped it. They listened to the sudden bangs of the farmer's automatic gun which scared off the pigeons. They collected beech mast and wood anemones and sycamore seedlings.

For the first hour the parson showed them things. But after that they found everything for themselves. One of the teachers accompanying the group said, 'We came through this wood yesterday but all we saw there was trees.'

We spent precious days scraping for pennies when we could have been better employed in educating. We felt like the medical people in tropical countries who know that a shilling can buy the penicillin to cure a child of yaws but can't get the shilling. It is the more exasperating when the people who have refused you the shilling make speeches extolling the virtues of penicillin.

We asked the Education Committee if they would allow us to buy, out of our annual allocation of money, a desk computer costing £40, pointing out the value of the computer and the fact that we would order fewer mathematics text-books if we got the computer. But the Committee said 'No'. When a woman member of a Dundee rationalist association read about this in a newspaper, she sent us a cheque for £40. The computer quickly proved its value. At first its novelty made pupils play with it for an hour at a time, finding what it could do. Out of this practice came a new understanding of arithmetical processes. For example, they discovered, quite on their own and without assistance from the teacher, that multiplication is repeated addition; and then that division is repeated subtraction. They began to think about what counting means, instead of dully following primary school drills.

We sent our pupils for a day a week gliding, in the months when the gliding station wasn't very busy. Some of the pupils had included this study in the work they were doing for the Duke of Edinburgh Award. For our youngsters, aiming at the Bronze Award, this meant proficiency in ground handling of gliders, launching procedures, signalling, the pre-flight cockpit check, and instrument reading and setting. It meant also five instructional flights, a knowledge of the rules of the air, and making a model glider and using it to demonstrate normal flight, the stall and the effect of trim changes.

Being under sixteen, our pupils were not permitted to go solo. On each visit to the airfield they got one flight. But they were kept busy throughout the day driving the tractor and assisting in the routine of launching. They took a responsible part in this drill, realizing that safety was involved and that the more efficiently the drill was carried out, the more the flights that would be launched. Pupils labelled 'difficult' in school (which sometimes means that they are not so docile as their fellows), pupils who resisted attempts to teach them quadratic equations or the exports of the Philippines and who, strangely enough, took no interest in the marital adventures of Henry VIII, sprang into lively activity when faced with the launching drill. Their instructors, members of the school staff (able glider pilots with a background of service experience, and not easily pleased), were delighted with the reactions of the pupils.

Flying was the thing. Then, when the delighted and fearful shock and thrill of the first flight was broadening into a relaxed understanding of the requirements of successful gliding, the instructors introduced the classroom work. But flying came first.

We asked the pupils to write down how they felt on their first flight. Nearly all of them were, before the trip, 'sort of nervous' or had 'butterflies in my stomach', and had the feeling of having their stomachs coming out of their mouths as they were being launched into the air. They all enjoyed the smoothness when the cable was released and they were airborne and independent of ground ties. One boy wrote, 'It was the most exciting thing I have done. The first thing you feel when you climb into the cockpit is of being scared but when you have been reassured that it will be all right, it is better. The instructor tells you how to manoeuvre the glider and then you are hauled up. Once you have released the cable it is quite a feeling to be dependent on yourself. When the glider dives you get a funny feeling but it was a very good day.'

As an English teacher I was interested to see if the pupils would be able to put vividly on paper a new and memorable experience. Most Scottish primary schools are absorbed in teaching pupils the rules of writing and they damp down or indeed quench a youngster's delight in the bright ring of words. I have often thought about the contrast between the wooden, lifeless and timid way in which they handle written words and the confidence and enjoyment with which they handle paint. I had put the contrast down to the fact that primary schools do so little art that pupils come to the secondary school without any prejudice against a paint brush. I had thought that if teachers in the primary school wearied pupils with art as much as they now do with English, then their paintings would be as dull as their writing. But a distinguished Scottish poet told me that using words is quite different from using paint and, if I understood him right, that you can't hope to use words vividly until you have served an apprenticeship in the feel and relationship and value of words, in the craft of writing. This is a question to which I hope we shall be one day able to give a clearer answer. In the meantime here is part of an account written by one of the boys:

After the signal was given to the winch, the glider started to move. Then it left the ground and soared into the air. The glider rose steadily, until it reached the length of the cable, the cable was released and the glider rose gracefully like a huge bird over Loch Leven. There was a wonderful view of a few islands sticking out of the mist. You thought the plane was hardly moving. It turned gently sideways towards the hill. It flew over the airfield, turned, and landed smoothly. Each of us handled the controls, and flew the glider. It was great.

As a contrast, here are extracts from what the girls wrote. One of them, who, the instructor said, had what seemed like a natural gift for flying and handled the controls with relaxed understanding, wrote this:

What I found very extraordinary was how long the wire stretched which pulls the glider into the air. I never would have believed it but when I was in the air I didn't want to go back down again.

Another girl wrote:

The views were lovely. We saw swans flying overhead and also boys bringing in the turnips in the fields below us.

Back in school, the pupils learn something of the theory of flight. It is no longer a remote, academic question, how a body which is heavier than air can stay in the air for so long. The study of the weather becomes relevant. If it's your day for gliding, the approach of depressions, warm or cold fronts, the forecasting of the weather, is something intimately intertwined with your happiness. If you want to become a good glider pilot, you have to try to learn about thermals, from a few short lessons, as much as a seagull gets out of a life's experience. And experience of gliding gives the pupil the ability to envisage the third dimension when he looks at a map. When he looks down on Fife from a thousand feet and sees Loch Leven and Kinross, roads and a railway and cars and farms and woods and a river, and the Lomond Hills strangely flat-looking from that height, he may begin to take a new, lively interest in maps, seeing them not as diagrams but as a kind of bird's-eye view (or glider's-eye view) of the earth beneath. And it is a wonderful experience for a fourteen-year-old pupil to see a large part of his home county not as a series of snapshots taken from a bus run or a cycle run, diminishing in clarity the farther it gets from the main road, but as a whole, and to realize that this is the part of the earth's wrinkled surface on which he has his being.

Coleridge said that it was one of the functions of poetry to let people see things freshly and with a sense of wonder. He could have said the same of education. We have to use everything that lies to our hand to tell our pupils of the earth's wonders. Our pupils, playing with the computer, had discovered what was for them a new truth, that multiplication is merely repeated addition. Gliding has a similar effect, and after even one trip, they return to school seeing life with a new freshness. And I think that getting their heads into the clouds once in a while has helped them to put their feet more firmly on the ground.

Chapter Two
The Pupils

One day I heard that the majority of the girls in the senior girls' class had arranged to meet in a public park after dark and have a thorough-going fight. I went to the class and pointed out that since their intention was presumably public knowledge, the police were likely to know – and to be in attendance. And that consequently it would be silly to go ahead with their plans. They listened politely. Next morning I asked two of the girls if they had had their fight at the public park as arranged.

'No' they replied, 'we didn't go to the park.' They paused. 'We went to the shore instead, to have our fight. Nobody interrupted.'

'What happened?'

'Well, the two sides lined up opposite one another and each of us had somebody to fight.'

'Who did you fight against?'

'Eleanor.'

'And you, Janet?'

'I fought against Mary.'

I tried to picture the scene. The light of a half-moon, the roar of the waves, ships on the Forth, lights along the bay and faintly the lights of Edinburgh on the other side of the Firth, the derelict lifeboat station, piles of rubbish on the shore, people sitting on coal bags in the condemned houses. But curiously at night (as thirty years ago it was by day) a beautiful scene. And there they were, these girls, tearing into one another in a series of single combats like the clan fight at the North Inch of Perth. I couldn't make head or tail of it, and asked, 'What happened then?'

'Well, we fought for a while. Then we all stopped and burst out laughing, and cleaned ourselves up. Then we wandered off home.'

'You mean you were all the best of friends after that?'

'Oh, yes.'

'So that you don't feel you want to go and fight one another again.'

'No.'

'Till next time.'

'I suppose so.'

I sent for a girl who had played truant for an afternoon. (There is what the newspapers call a 'human story' behind almost all the reports that I have to inquire into.) She is an attractive reliable girl, and slowly the story came out. Three years previously at Dundee her mother had bought her an expensive piece of cloth to make a doll's dress. Every now and again during these years Carol asked her mother when she was going to help to cut out the doll's dress, and her mother, who goes out to work, said, 'As soon as I've time.' At last Carol took scissors and cut out the dress herself, and made a mess of it, and realized the cost of her mistake. She didn't dare tell her mother. Her father is a miner, working at the coal-face, and he has a good wage. Carol doesn't take school dinners at a shilling a day; she goes out for a meal which costs 3s. 6d. By doing without her midday meal for a fortnight she saved 35s., which was almost the cost of the cloth. But she couldn't go and buy new cloth on a Saturday because her mother doesn't work on a Saturday and is therefore more able to check up on Carol's movements. So Carol took an afternoon off school to go to a neighbouring town and buy material to substitute for the material she had spoiled.

One thing I have learned is the importance of keeping one's mind open to a different interpretation of the facts. Carol's story was true, and I made a mental picture of her mother. The picture was wrong, as I discovered when the mother called several months later to pay her share of a school expedition in which Carol was to take part. 'Carol's father spoils her,' she said. 'Her father lets her do what she likes and I wonder if that's good for her. Oh, I dinna ken. I just want to do the best I can for her.'

This was not the mother I had imagined, but an open, friendly, considerate woman, fond of her daughter. She wondered if it was a good thing for Carol that she herself, disliking housework, went out to work five days a week. Lots of parents are similarly unsure of their attitudes, having themselves broken away from the restrictions of their own upbringing, wishing to have a good life for themselves and aware of the higher standard of living that a double pay coming into the house brings with it, and at the same time wondering what is the best way to bring up children. But this, I think, is a sound and healthy situation, when people, admitting their mistakes and their uncertainties, try to find their own answers to their own questions instead of applying the ideas of an earlier generation to a new set of circumstances.

Another mother came to the school when I asked her to, because her son had been stealing coal from the school's supply. She came in with an angry, but tired, attitude. 'This is a terrible thing to say about a laddie of twelve,' she said. 'He has never been in trouble in his life.' I told her of the reports of the people who had seen this after-dark raid by children on the school's coal, and she went away. She returned next day and said the boy had admitted it. 'Poor laddie,' she said, 'he knew how short of coal we are and he just did it because he thought he was helping me.'

She told me the story of the family. Her husband was out of work because of recurrent illness. The mother herself was having a wearing struggle to keep the family going. The children who were at school were rosy-cheeked, but she herself was under-nourished and tired. (A year later she died, and the family was broken up between different institutions and relatives.)

Every week brings its story. A boy of fourteen is absent most Mondays. We inquire and find that his mother is an invalid and his father's wages are small and he does the washing and ironing on Mondays. A doctor phones to ask if a girl of thirteen may be allowed two afternoons off to help her widowed mother who is going next month to have a cardiac operation. A foster mother comes to talk about a fourteen-year-old girl in her care who has suddenly begun to kick over the traces.

A father, separated from his wife, came to take his twelve-year-old daughter to live with him in Birmingham. I asked her if she wanted to go. She replied, 'I don't know. You see, I don't remember him at all.' But she went south with him. A year later she returned. The Birmingham school report on the girl said she was 'unstable'. It was not surprising.

Most of the parents are comfortably well-off. Many of them

run big cars. The pupils look sturdy, well-fed and well-dressed. Very few are under-nourished; the welfare state has seen to that. A comparison of the Coal Town pupils of thirty years ago with today's pupils emphasizes the extent of the social revolution. Nobody can have anything but praise and admiration for the people whose work has brought this revolution about. Looking at these six hundred at the morning assembly in the school hall, I think often what a fine-looking lot they are. But that does not prevent doubt and confusion. The pupils are all dressed up but neither they, nor their parents, know where they are going.

Anna is fourteen. She is highly intelligent. She passed her eleven plus and went to the senior secondary school. Her father and mother couldn't get on together. The father occasionally escaped from rows at home by going on huge binges, ending up by breaching the peace and being taken in the Black Maria to the police cells. Anna's older sister, also at the senior secondary school, began to steal. Perhaps a psychiatrist would have said that the stealing was due to her disturbed state, but she didn't get the chance to see a psychiatrist. (Concerning another pupil a psychiatrist said, 'I ought to see him every two days but we are terribly understaffed and I can only see him once a month.') She appeared at the juvenile court. Children can be just as cruel as adults and the eleven plus élite of pupils at the senior secondary school took it out on Anna. There was her father in the cells. And her sister on probation. Anna couldn't stand the spoken criticism and the imagined insults and began to play truant. Then she fell behind in her exam marks and pressure was put on her to do better, by teachers who knew that her work didn't measure up to her ability. As a result of all this pressure she refused to attend school. All the machinery of persuasion and compulsion was set in motion but she resisted it. It is one of the more attractive features of our society's educational system that it is prepared to admit defeat rather than have recourse to the heavier pressures, and finally Anna was asked to attend the Coal Town school. She agreed.

Here she escaped from the examination pressure, and the comparison with the home backgrounds of other pupils. Even when things got worse at home she still came to school because she could relax. Her mother left home and went to work in Glasgow; but then felt the tug of the children's affection and returned. But there continued to be frequent rows between the parents, and the father threatened to leave.

If we had followed dutifully the dictates of the Scottish Education Department we would have tried to force Anna through the O-grade examination hoop, testing her knowledge of Australian rainfall and the history of the Scottish Church, of algebra and calories. But one of the women members of the staff took a special interest in her and became a friend. Anna told her about the bad days and also told her when she felt like running away from home, but said she couldn't really run away because what would happen to her little sister. In Anna, the teacher found a maturity of judgement beyond her years and a readiness to shoulder responsibility. She loved both her parents although they didn't love one another.

I don't know if it was too late for the parents to begin their social education, to learn that, like swimming, living happily together is a skill that improves by taking thought over it. Certainly the social services were overburdened and there was really nobody who could give to the parents the time and attention they would need if they were to make a go of it. But I think Anna was beginning to learn something of all this. That is not the proper way to put it. Rather all that we were doing was giving her the relaxed background against which the human understanding she had possessed all the time might have peace to flourish. When she grows up she will be a good citizen and will make a good and a happy home. Without benefit of the O-grade examinations.

I think life is harder now for young people than it has been for fifty years. There are the greater examination pressures in the schools. There are more broken homes. Mothers of young children go out to work – six million of them in Britain. Children who are ill are sent to school so that mother won't miss a shift. One curious feature of this new situation is the emergence of the 'gran' (grandmother) as the prop and mainstay in many Coal Town families. Many pupils speak in respectful and affectionate terms of their 'gran'. In the days when (as it must seem to many children) the heavens are falling, the grans are saving the sum of things, unpaid. Some of them are still quite young and strong and enjoy their new responsibilities and place in society; they are glad to be felt to be needed. Others, older and rather tired, respond nobly, but I sometimes think it is unfair to ask a woman who has worked hard and brought up a family to take over a second brood when she is older and would rather be taking life more easily.

An official came to the school to visit Peter, aged thirteen. From the time he was nine till he was twelve, Peter was in an approved school, but the school gave him up as a bad job and sent him back to the ordinary school where we tried to cope with him as best we could. He shouted at the teachers words that the rest of the pupils regarded as unspeakable – in school, anyway – and he showed off for much of the time. The teachers bit their tongues in an effort to give him a chance to get it out of his system. All this was played down in the report about him which the school had to send to the juvenile court when he appeared on a charge of destroying a brick wall. That incident occurred on the day the circus came to the town. They were going to unload the elephants at the station and Peter as usual was in the forefront of the spectators. But it was a long time before the elephants appeared, and Peter and his pals put in the waiting time knocking down what remained of a tumbledown brick wall.

The juvenile court magistrates were lenient and Peter remained at the school. Later we sent him with a small group, mountain climbing in Glen Lyon. It had worked before, so why not with Peter? But Peter continued his trail of damage in the Highlands. The freedom of the hills had had no effect that we could see.

Back in school he started running a protection racket. It was our bad luck that he had an answer for the specific instance on which we questioned him. He had not, it seemed, ever threatened this particular boy; the boy paid up without being threatened.

Later a teacher pointed out to the class that it was time they took a stand against Peter. They did. They gave him hell. After a bit I spoke to the class. With that ready generosity of children which is one of the bright things that keeps us going when we are just about giving up hope, they called off their campaign and gave Peter a break.

Eager to believe that we were getting somewhere, we began to put some store on the slightest reports of an improvement that reached us from outside the school. And in school, too, things were not so bad. I watched him at the Christmas party, putting everything he knew into mastering the steps of the Canadian Barn Dance, his hair beautifully oiled and his tie straight. But after Christmas there was more trouble.

'Do you realize,' I asked him, 'that if I pick up the phone you could be sent back to the Approved School? Do you want to go back to the Approved School?'

'No,' he said.

The following afternoon he damaged some lavatory fittings. It looked like the end of the road. But in a school you can never be sure. Half a dozen pupils, no friends of Peter, gave evidence that an older and more intelligent pupil had dared Peter to do the damage, and he'd accepted the dare to maintain his prestige. But a month later, after a classroom scene in which Peter, right in the middle of the picture, had shouted insulting words at a woman teacher, I did pick up the phone and the official arrived. I sent for Peter.

'Do you realize that you can be taken back to an Approved School at any time?' the official asked him. 'You are still on licence, you know.' Peter looked blankly unhappy, but didn't answer, and the official continued, 'The authorities are beginning to lose their patience with people like you that cause so much trouble. You needn't think you'll be sent back to the same Approved School where you slept in a dormitory. This time you'll be sent to a new Approved School where you'll have a cell to sleep in. Do you want to be sent away from home again?' There was no answer at first. Peter's eyes showed the clouded doubt that he was trying to see through, to give an answer. 'I don't know,' he said at length.

'Why don't you know?'

'Well, last night . . .' And here the words began to tumble out, angrily,' . . . last night four and elevenpence disappeared from the mantelpiece and my mother blamed me. It's always me that gets the blame. I never saw the four and elevenpence. I don't know who took it.'

In a considerate way the official helped Peter to the answer he was struggling to give. 'And when something like that happens, you feel you would be as well away from home?'

'Yes, sir.'

'But on the whole you'd rather stay at home?'

'Yes, sir.'

'I'm told that you have a job at week-ends delivering rolls and that you're saving up money to go with a school party mountain-climbing in the Highlands.'

'Yes, sir.'

'How much have you saved?'

'I'm starting saving next week-end.'

'How much do you have to save?'

'Three pounds to go to the Highlands for a month.'

'Well, Peter, I'll tell you what I'll do. When you've saved two pounds and given it to your headmaster, I'll add the third pound. What do you say to that? Is it a bargain?'

'Yes, sir.'

'When will you bring your first savings to the school office?'

'Next Monday. I'll bring half a crown.'

He was as good as his word. And the following Monday he brought another half-crown. But on the Tuesday he came to say could he have one-and-six out of his account so that he could join a bus party that was going to watch a local first division team play a European team. I said no and he left, but a woman teacher who was present offered to give him the money and Peter was called back. When he received it, he stood uncertain and then suddenly shot out his hand. The teacher shook it. Next day I asked him if he had enjoyed the match. He replied, unexpectedly, 'It was a lovely match' but he never paid any more into his account. It stood at five shillings.

A mother came to the school to ask what chance her daughter had of being transferred to the High School. Her older daughter, she told me, was in her final year there and likely to do very well in her 'Highers' (the Scottish Education Department's certificate examination). I asked her, 'Is it so important that Janey should go to the High School?'

She paused and then said quietly. 'I see what you mean. Maybe you're right. Her older sister is in and out of the doctor's surgery all the time, with her nerves. The doctor said she passed her eleven plus on phenobarbitones. Janey's different since she came here. I don't know how much she's learning, but she's a nicer lassie in the house. Easy to get on with and ready to help. She's happy here. She's pleased with life and she's well.'

'I see what you mean.' I said, 'Maybe you can pay too big a price for the Highers.'

She replied, 'Aye, that's so.'

Another day a father stormed into the school, blazing with anger because, he said, his son had been belted without reason. The teacher told me his side of the story. Then I sent for the boy and, in the presence of the parent, asked him if he agreed with the teacher's account of the incident. He agreed.

I have often been amazed at the truthfulness and courage of children if they feel they are going to get a fair deal. I had talked to this boy quietly and asked if he would give me his version, because my job was to be fair to the teacher and fair to him. Although he knew that his words would disappoint and deflate his father, since the incident hadn't been quite as the father had imagined (the pupil having told him only one side of the story), he told the truth.

His father turned on him angrily and said, 'That wasna what you told me last night.'

'I know,' said the boy.

'Well, if you'd said that last night, I'd never have come up here the day. You've made me feel stupid.'

The boy didn't answer. It was a situation I'd met before but I'm always surprised when I meet it, because it is so different from an adult's reaction. Caught out like this, an adult would bluster so as not to lose face.

The boy returned to his classroom. The parent gave me his confidence. 'It's like this,' he said, 'I was brought up in an institution. Every night for years I wet the bed. And every morning I was belted for it. But I couldna help it. I tried not to, and I couldna help it. And I made up my mind that no child of mine would ever be belted if I could stop it.'

One day I had a visit from a mother. She had had an illegitimate son, and later married and her husband had died. She herself was teetering on the edge of being taken away to a mental hospital. She was afraid, not so much of the hospital, although that scared her too, but of losing her son. It must be a frightening thing to feel that the authorities may be able to prove that you are not a fit and proper person to be in charge of your son. She said, 'Will you help me? Will you see that they don't take me away to a mental hospital?' I got a glimpse of an awful loneliness, a lone individual hopelessly facing (to her) hostile society. Is this the twentieth-century version of an ancient pattern? I imagine this is how a woman felt long ago when she was faced with a charge of witchcraft and the impossibility of proving that she was *not* a witch.

In our organized society, the individual can be very lonely, and among the loneliest and bleakest lives are those of people whose sanity has come in doubt. This is a situation where it is most difficult of all to trust yourself when all men doubt you, because, I suppose, everybody does irrational things and once you begin to consider your sanity, you can easily find reason for doubt about yourself. Then comes the problem of establishing your sanity and proving it. A problem which, mercifully, few people are faced with. In the present state of the law it is much too easy for the individual to be 'put away' (although temporarily); it needs only the say-so of two doctors, one of whom may be no expert in these things.

There's a curious dichotomy in this. What I've written about a lonely woman fighting against the machinery of society is true; but it isn't the whole truth. When her husband died, three probation officers had worked many evenings in their spare time cleaning out the dirty, smelly house, scrubbing, painting and papering it. When her son brought his pals, all twelve-year-olds like himself, into the house and broke windows and fittings and made much noise and neighbours complained, the Town Council, understanding the situation, were very patient indeed. The doctors couldn't have been kinder to her. She had no money to give the boy pocket-money and he stole from her. When she tried to keep her purse from him, he hit her, on several occasions, with any weapon that came handy.

A local church (although she had no connexion with it) pro-

vided £2 10s. to help the school send the boy with a group that
was to spend ten days at the school's cottage at Loch Rannoch.
Up on the mountains for the first days the boy talked incessantly
with nervous energy. Then he quietened down. One day the group
set out to cross a high pass from Rannoch to Glen Lyon. They
carried tents to sleep two. The boy was a bed-wetter and none
of the others would share a tent with him, so they pitched their
tents beside a ruined cottage and the boy slept in the cottage. At
1 a.m. on a quiet winter's night he got up and wakened the
teacher in charge, and on the verge of tears told him, 'Sir, it's
spooky in there.' Another boy put his head out of his tent and
said, 'Aye, sir, that's right. It must be spooky sleeping by yersel
in there. He can come into our tent.'

This other boy, heftier than the rest of the group, had been
running a protection racket in the school. 'Threepence or I'll
batter your face in.' When we heard about it, he had collected
over ten shillings from his frightened class-mates. We persuaded
him to pay it all back. This is one of the instances we come across
from time to time, not all that uncommon, that give us confidence
that the line we are taking is the right one, perhaps the only right
one – the fact that a bullying racketeer pushes his head out of a
tent in the darkness and offers to share his tent with a bed-wetter.

When the group returned to school, the teacher in charge told
me that this frightened boy had turned out to be an excellent
naturalist. I talked to him:

'How did you like the Rannoch expedition?'

'It was smashing.'

'You enjoyed it?'

'Yes.'

'I'm told you are interested in watching birds and animals.
You've learned quite a bit about them.'

'Yes.'

'What did you see?'

'Well, there was tree-creepers and capercailzies and sparrow-
hawks and kestrels and ptarmigan and, oh, lots of birds.'

'What's the difference between a sparrow-hawk and a kestrel?'

'Well, a kestrel's a browny colour, and a sparrow-hawk . . .
well, a sparrow-hawk looks fiercer.'

Two days later his mother came to the school. I was prepared to hear about the difference that ten days in the hills had made to her boy. She said, 'He's been much worse since he came back home.'

'What's happened?'

'There's no holding him. He shouts and swears and gets his pals to shout at me, and they are breaking up the house.'

Later I sent for the boy and tried to find out what was behind all this. At first he wouldn't speak. Then he broke out, 'Well, she just nags and nags and nags, and I just lifted a broom and hit her.'

The teacher who had been in charge of the Rannoch group sympathized with the boy. He said, 'He had freedom up in Rannoch. Then he comes back and he finds himself held in at every turn. So he lashes out. Isn't it understandable?'

I suppose it is. But it is understandable also that his mother, worried about many things, frightened of being put out of the house, of being accused of not being able to control her son and his pals, should nag at him.

Another day the mother came to tell me that the boy had refused to get up unless she gave him pocket money. Finally he had thrown a pot of tea against the new wallpaper and hit her with a broom. Then out in the street he had called her a 'bag' and a 'cow'. I talked to the boy, telling him that at the age of twelve he was at a turning point of his life. If he wanted to be sent away to a children's home, this was the way to go about it, to continue to act as he was doing. If he wanted to stay with his mother, he would have to behave differently towards her. Did he want to stay with his mother? With surprising maturity he replied, 'She's difficult to live with but, yes, I'd want to stay with her. I don't want to be separated from her.' I asked him if he was fond of his mother. He considered the question and said he was.

The following week he was cutting up the linoleum of the living room with a knife. On such occasions he seemed to be unaware of the results of his actions, to be pathologically lacking in even immediate foresight. And so the situation continues and worsens. 'Is there no balm in Gilead? Is there no physician there?'

We had him in the school office. He was pleased to go errands and be selected for this job. He turned up at school with his face washed and his hair smoothed back and shining. His mother said he had complained about his Wellington boots, which at that time were the only footwear he had. He felt that they were not appropriate for his office job. He delivered his messages intelligently and eagerly and smilingly. Probably we should have kept him in the office. We're like the rest of the traditionalists – we're too readily impressed by the people who say, 'But look at the education he's missing.' We sent him back to his class. He became troublesome again. He wouldn't come to school unless his mother gave him pocket money, but she hadn't any to give him. She used to go out into the street and get his pals to try and persuade him out of his bed, but their help was of no use. Then he'd got a gun and shot slugs into his mother's legs and the probation officer took him away to a children's home in another area. From there he wrote to me, 'Send me letter and don't forget for it is so deliting.'

Chapter Three
The Theory

What should a Coal Town school be doing to help these pupils find some sense of direction in their journey through life? Assuredly something very different from what is being done at present throughout the length and breadth of Britain. Education is too serious a matter to be left entirely to the professional educationists. It would be a good thing if the great majority of people started inquiring into education, taking policy out of the hands of the experts, and basing it not on tradition but on their own ideas of what is the best way to prepare a child for life and for making a living. The system has become so out of touch with living conditions that it is no longer feasible to patch and repair it. It needs remaking from the foundation – starting with the whole purpose of having schools at all. This book is an attempt to persuade people to start out on their own and decide for themselves what education is about. Then, when we see clearly the purpose of having schools, it should not be beyond our ability to carry out in these schools the kind of work which aims at achieving that purpose.

Like the teenagers, education has lost its way. What happened in the last century was something like this. Such little education as there was outside the grammar and public schools was due to a mixture of genuine benevolence (which showed sporadically through nineteenth-century laissez-faire economics like green patches on a snow-covered mountain), fear that the poor would start a revolution (and that was partly why religious teaching was emphasized), and the need to supervsie children whose mothers were working in factories. The Acts of the decade between 1870 and 1880 brought into schools unprepared for them a large number of children who hadn't been at school before, and there was much unintelligent cramming of the three Rs. Until 1902 it was illegal to spend ratepayers' money on secondary education, and when at length secondary education was extended to a wider public, there wasn't the fundamental inquiry one would have expected into the kind of curriculum which this big new development demanded. Instead, it was the grammar and public school curriculum which was followed which was not greatly different from the curriculum of the year 1500, being based largely on Latin and Greek. Some other subjects had been grudgingly introduced. Mathematics had been permitted entry, provided it wasn't concerned with practical things but was of the nature of Euclid which, like Latin, was held to have more educational value than anything else because 'it teaches you to think'. The story of education is a story of unexamined assumptions, and this is one of them.

A whole complex of emotions has surrounded the educational system. In Scotland particularly, working folk treated education with reverence. Many parents, including my own, saved and denied themselves many of the luxuries of life, and some of its necessities, in order that their children could go to the universities. It was not their fault that they were not in a position to assess the value of the education for which they sacrificed so much. My father, whose sayings linger in my ears as freshly as if they had been spoken yesterday, quoted the Proverbs, 'With all thy getting, get understanding', and that is as near to the whole purpose of education as anyone is likely to get. He could not know that what we were doing at school and university was mostly memorizing information, a very different thing.

On the whole, many people outside education accept the idea that the educationists know what they are doing and that it has all been thoroughly gone into and considered, and modified in the light of experience. But it is not like that at all. History is taught this way because it has always been taught this way. It is based on a faith that somehow this information about Charles II is good for you, that somehow it makes you a better citizen, and there goes with it a kind of hope that at a future general election these teenagers will sit down reflectively and, in the light of their knowledge of the constitutional issues raised by the reign of Charles II, decide whom to vote for. But what, in fact, happens in the classroom is that the teacher dictates to the pupils model answers to the likely questions, and the pupils copy down the answers and learn them by heart. When the examination is over, the answers are forgotten.

But it is not only in what are called the cultural subjects that there is this lack of connexion between means and ends. Similarly unrelated to any life the pupils will live are the questions, for example, in the navigation paper. The Scottish Education Department, rightly disappointed at the small number of Scottish schools which teach sea-navigation, sent a circular to the schools urging those that are on the coast to consider introducing navigation. The Coal Town was once a fishing village, before coal was discovered under the town, and many of its people, as they look out over the Forth and watch Granton trawlers, Leith cargo-boats, Grangemouth tankers, and destroyers and submarines from Rosyth pass up and down, feel a hankering for the sea, a longing to revert to an ampler life. I thought it would be a good thing to encourage pupils to be at home out in the Firth, in boats, and I requested a specialist to visit the school and discuss how to set about it. Even if the pupils worked all their lives in coal tunnels under the Forth, it would be a good thing for them to sail their own boats in their leisure time.

But the specialist wasn't helpful. His conversation was of charts and declination and astro-navigation, all classroom work. I suggested that the first thing to do was to get a boat, and I asked if the Department could help us by telling us what was the best kind of boat for our purpose and for the special conditions of sailing on the Forth; and if they had any contacts with the Navy or the Merchant Navy, and could recommend an ex-sailor who would be good with the pupils and also thoroughly reliable at sea with a young crew. The Department was not prepared to offer any advice on these points. The inspector said that there was much value to be got out of a navigation course, even if you never got a boat. And there was the crux of the matter, for it seems to me that is where the inspector and the Department are completely wrong. What they are saying is that mental activity is in itself so valuable that it forms the greater part of education. But we in the school were trying to tackle education from quite another point of view. For us the main thing was to get pupils out in a boat, and the main reasons for the classroom work in navigation was to teach them what to do if things went wrong in the Firth; if, for example a fog came down and they lost their way. We are never likely to be well-enough off to be able to buy the kind of boat with a cabin containing a roomy table where pupils could undertake the complexities of chart-work which form the basis of the O-Grade Scottish Certificate of Education examination in navigation. From experience as a navigator in Bomber Command during the war, I knew how inaccurate astro-navigation was, and that our pupils, bobbing up and down in a fishing yawl between Fife Ness and Dunbar, were unlikely to add anything to their knowledge of where they were from looking up astro-navigation tables.

The great advantage of chart-work and astro-navigation and these things, from the Education Department's point of view, is that it is so easily examinable. John Smith gets 68 per cent and James Thomson gets 75 per cent and down go these accurate-seeming figures in the report that will be sent to the prospective employer. But the value to these boys of going out in a boat and gradually gaining confidence in their ability to meet with emergencies and to pull out everything they've got in the fight with nature – that value is not so accurately measurable.

The people mainly responsible, the members of the education departments, when you meet them individually and in situations where they can speak freely and off the record, are sensible, sympathetic, understanding people, aware of the small impact that official education is making on the life of the Coal Town. Why is it that the contribution of these people to national life, as an official department, is so much less in value than one would have supposed from one's knowledge of them individually? One explanation was given by a distinguished industrialist who has done as much as anybody to revitalize the sagging economy of Scotland. 'Many of our troubles come from the knighthoods which crown a successful career in a government department. They encourage men to play safe. I have known able people who played an energetic part in public life. After they joined the Civil Service we never had a cheep out of them.'

That may be part of the truth. But there is a more likely reason for the failure of these members of the education departments to put into effective action their own ideas on education. They have not been themselves given the kind of education which would have helped them strenuously and confidently to take hold of the machine and make it serve the needs of children.

I used to wonder why in the Middle Ages the Inquisition persisted in spite of the fact that there must have been many humane priests. The reason possibly is that the machine was too much for them, too.

Chapter Four
The Practice

This being so, what had we to do, in the Coal Town School, to make the machine work for our youngsters, and not against them?

To begin with, we had to ask ourselves what culture usually meant in the schools. It meant the O-grade certificate. It meant a detailed knowledge of the *Ancient Mariner*. A detailed knowledge of sentence analysis, parts of speech, prosody.

A former pupil came to see me because she wasn't making a success of the course in cookery she was doing at a technical college in another part of the country. I said that her mother was an excellent cook and could help her. Her older sister had made a success of the course. Couldn't she help? The girl replied, 'But it's not the cookery that worries me. I'm getting on all right with it.'

'Well, what *is* it that's worrying you?'

'It's . . . it's the *prepositions*.'

The more alterations we made in our school work, the more did it become apparent that we had done no more than make a beginning. I began to be forced back to the conclusion that there was very little in the curriculum which could defend its right to inclusion. The mathematics department, for example, admitted that the only reason for much of their work was that it was *English* – it explained to pupils the vocabulary of shapes. They understood the meaning of rhombus, equilateral, right angle, circumference, ratio, hypotenuse, trapezium, parallel, congruent, cone, equation and many such terms. I could see both boys and girls drawing circles and devising circular patterns, measuring angles and acquiring skill in calculations, and liking the work; and in so doing increasing their vocabulary of shapes. But I am not convinced that it adds up to very much. A government report on the teaching of mathematics said that 'through constructive play, experiment and discussion children become aware of relationships and develop mental structures which are mathematical in form.' But this is surely an attempt, by blurring meaning, to give permanence to a concept that evaporates as you consider it – 'mental structures which are mathematical in form.'

One of our teachers tried to find out, no easy task, why a pupil disliked theoretical mechanics. He discovered that the reason was probably that the boy was 'all at sea'. He didn't know what they were talking about. For example, he could work out sums on the moments of a force, but he had no idea what the moments of a force were. Mechanics teachers use a phrase like that partly because it is a handy, short phrase but chiefly, I believe, because it sounds professional. There's a glamour about a specialized vocabulary, making the user thank God that he is not as other men who can't use it. A teacher can't afford to fall for this glamour. If he is to make a success of his job he must go for simplicity and resist the exotic charms of dolled-up words. In this instance the teacher should go into the words 'moment' and 'momentum' (which I suppose just mean 'movement') and explain the connexion between movement and time. Similarly, when I was thirteen, a mathematics teacher spoke with easy familiarity about 'the function of x' as if we were on as friendly terms with the word 'function' as with (say) the word 'dumpling'. I remember being slightly perturbed about this because all the other pupils seemed to know what it meant; at any rate nobody asked any questions about it. At last I steeled myself to risk a laugh, and I put up my hand and asked what the word 'function' meant. The teacher went to much trouble to explain it. Now, did I see it? No, I didn't. He continued the explanation. Now was it clear? No, it wasn't. The teacher tried a third time, very patiently. By now the class was taking an amused interest in the teacher's efforts to cope with my failure of understanding. So, when the teacher reached the end of the third exposition, and said, '*Now* do you get it?' I capitulated and said 'Yes'. But I still don't see why it is necessary to press-gang the word 'function' into this very specialized mathematical activity. Surely there is a simpler way of putting it?

The artificiality of all this at first baffles pupils, and then they write it off as having no relation to anything. An Aberdeenshire farmer told me a story about this. One morning he showed his grieve a very large field that had to be manured and gave him the supply of sacks of artificial manure all ready. When he returned in the evening he found that a considerable part of the field had not been manured. The supply had run out before they reached it, the grieve said. 'But,' the farmer said, 'you knew that this is a twenty-acre field. Therefore you could have worked out what area each sack of manure would have to cover. There are 4840 square yards in an acre. You knew that.'

'God almichty,' said the grieve, 'they learned us that at the school, but I never thocht it would be of any use to me.'

One of the favourite questions in history examinations is about the unification of Italy. Throughout Britain at this moment children are memorizing a sentence which says that 'Cavour achieved more by diplomacy than Garibaldi by all his victories.' Few teachers stop to explain clearly what Cavour was doing when he was being diplomatic. (Few teachers know how diplomats spend their time.) I try to picture Cavour a century ago in a palace in Rome. Was it just that he was a friendly, open man who got people to trust him and to agree to his proposals for treaties? Or was he a smart Alec like the hire-purchase man at the door who gets you to put your signature to an agreement before you've understood or even read it? Or is the world 'diplomacy' a euphemism? Did Cavour fill his guests full of Frascati wine and send them off to luxurious beds made comfortable by the presence of a warm contadina? If there had been a modern popular newspaper in 1861, a *Roman Daily Courier*, its gossip columns would have satisfied our curiosity about some of these things.

This use of unexplained words and concepts is one of the sad results of the pressure of written examinations. There are no premiums of marks for the pupils whose teacher takes them on revealing and rewarding rambles down the by-ways of understanding. These side tracks are time-consuming and the teacher has much ground to cover for the examination. The pupils memorize these imposing words (moment, function, diplomacy and the rest of them) and gallop on because there is no time to be lost. The teacher has not made clear to the pupil the content of meaning of these words; he has left too much for the imagination of the pupil to fill in; the pupil has not himself the background of experience on which to draw in order to fill in the meaning. The teacher is not using words as they could be used, and the pupil gets the feeling that words have small value, that they are inefficient tools. The teacher has devalued the currency of words.

Together with too little attention to the significance of individual words goes too great attention to the machinery of fitting words together. Pupils get detailed knowledge about analysis (an adult study) and parts of sentences are labelled with elaborate technical terms like 'predicate'. I've never understood what the word 'predicate' really means, or indeed why it is necessary to have such a word. But the children in most primary schools are taught to identify predicates. They learn to talk as glibly about predicates as about the function of x and the moments of a force. The writing of English is presented as an elaborate and artificial skill. Most pupils feel that it is not for them. They struggle to understand when the teacher patiently explains what a sentence is, and get confused as the centipede did that could walk perfectly until somebody asked it which leg moved after which. The idea of what a sentence is, is not necessary for a child. (You might as well ask what a word or a letter is.) The ablest of human beings haven't yet been able satisfactorily to analyse speech. Being a living thing, speech just will not fall neatly into the pattern drawn up for it by the grammarians. Some teachers say that you use a full stop to show a pause in speech, but people run sentences together as Lewis Grassic Gibbon does in *Sunset Song* which better reflects what he calls the 'speak' of the people. It is surprising how easily the reader, although brought up to believe that the neatly-partitioned written sentences mirror normal speech, falls into the more idiomatic speech-like writing of Gibbon.

I believe that it is this complicated formal grammatical education that inhibits writing when the pupils come to the secondary school. In Art our pupils have not been bemused with analyses and exercises in 'composition', and when they are given paper, paint and a paintbrush they fall to with glee and enjoy painting pictures and the results are good. They don't dare to splash words about as they splash paint.

People have been little disposed to question the studies imposed on children in state schools. When London became the mercantile centre of the world, geography and profit and loss arithmetic were thrust upon the maintained schools because clerks were wanted in large numbers. But long after these vocational requirements had largely dried up, children throughout Britain were working away at elaborate sums on compound interest. It was like the film of Laurel and Hardy still in their dugout in the trenches long after the war had stopped; nobody had told them.

As far as secondary modern children of our own day are concerned, what is the effect and what are the advantages of this bumbling educational tradition? Almost nil. The evidence grows that their ten years of desk-sitting make little positive impression on our pupils. All those sums and interpretation exercises, the causes and results of wars, the imports and exports – where has all the knowledge gone? Down the drain, mostly. If all our schools, primary and secondary, were wiped out tomorrow, apart from a little temporary inconvenience, the country would hardly know the difference.

At first, anyway. Later there would be such an upsurge of cultural interest, released from the pressure of school education, that half our major problems would be solved within a decade.

If you believe that this is exaggerated talk and that, if our primary and secondary schools were liquidated, our society and civilization would fall to the ground, let me tell you the story of Michael Macalister. He is a farmer in the remote part of the Highlands. The total time that Mike spent at school was one half day. This must be a British record. How he managed to get away with it I don't know, but it's true. Because of illness he didn't go to school until he was seven. Half a day was enough for him, perhaps because he didn't like being treated as a five-year-old. He didn't go back. An older brother who was at school taught him the elements of reading, writing and counting. Once he'd got the elements, Mike declined further refinements from his brother. Four brothers went to the university and got degrees. It was one of these who told me about Mike. They spend their holidays at his farm. One evening Mike was writing out an order for seed and manure, so much per acre and at such and such a rate. 'I'll get a pencil and paper and work this out,' said one of the educated brothers. He sat and figured it all out diligently, checking his working. When he'd finished, Mike, who was relaxing in the armchair at the fireside, said, 'I make it such and such.' The cost that he had worked out in his head was the same as the brother had reached in twice the time with pencil and paper. It just shows what a school education doesn't do for you.

One of Britain's best known scientists sometimes spends his holidays in that remote part of Scotland, but it is not the M.A. brothers he seeks out to talk to; it is Mike, whose mental agility and fresh unexpectedness and untutored responses he finds stimulating.

That's the trouble with the professional educationists; with their stock responses they've tutored the life out of their pupils and students. It was a member of this same family who told me about a Highland gamekeeper whom he had met back home when he was on holiday after he'd got a teaching job in another part of the country. The gamekeeper said, 'You know, I see all you fellows, fine strapping fellows, growing up here. And then you go off to Glasgow or somewhere to get your education. And then you become teachers. And then years later I see you back here for your holidays. And do you know what you look like? Do you know what you look like? You look like sookit oranges. *Sookit oranges.*'

Education, which should be a nourishing thing providing growth, is anything but that. It is a narrow thing, restricting growth. It is restricted in being largely confined to the severely intellectual, shutting out the sensuous side of things, denying the child's right to experience. And even within its own sphere, the intellectual, it denies freedom of thinking. The examination system which covers Britain like a Wellsian fungus throttles and chokes freedom of thought.

I asked a woman doctor what she remembered of her school education. She remembered a woman teacher of French who dressed with quiet elegance and always had her hair beautifully tended. She remembered this teacher telling them about the recurrence of the words for shade and shutters in French literature – *ombre* and *volet* – and the importance for people living in bright sunshine to escape from it. She remembered the teacher helping them to appreciate the rich fullness of the meaning of the word '*velour*', used to describe the surface of the skin of a peach.

Now why did these things spring so readily to memory when so much else had disappeared without trace? I think it is because our childhood longs for the sensuous richness of which it is largely starved; this food for touch and taste and sight and sound and experience.

You can't create a participant society (or indeed anything else) without imagination, a quality not much encouraged by the educational administrators because it is so difficult to put a percentage assessment on, for their files. (Another reason is perhaps that imagination is a quality in which children are much richer than adults.) Had we in the Coal Town School stumbled on an old truth, 'Except ye become as a little child, ye shall in no wise enter into the Kingdom of Heaven?' Was one of the corollaries of that theorem that without imagination you cannot create a participant society?

Certainly the most glaring fault of the educational system is its neglect of imagination. Therefore if we are going to create a participant society, the arts will have to be nourished in the school. And this is what we in the Coal Town had been trying to do, in the teeth of the Scottish Education Department and the County Council.

It started in the art room of the school, and years later spread to the English and music classrooms. It was a search for excellence, a love of doing things well, a self-forgetting absorption in putting every scrap of ability one possessed into a picture or a poem or a song. It was almost everything that the present system isn't. The state system makes a pupil work in order to get marks and passes; that is, it is a search for advantage, a self-based thing. Pressures are put on the pupil to work well, and with the pressures – strains. But if a pupil is engrossed in imaginative and creative work, although he is putting everything he knows into what he is doing, there is a sense of release in it. Here is a poem written by one of our pupils, a fourteen year old boy. It is called 'Fish Thinking'.

As I sat doing a play
this morning
My mind it ran backwards
I thought of fish running
uncannily through the water.

Its shape,
the dark movements of water
glowed in my mind. It was
as if I were there.
In my mind I was there, as if
I was the fish,
gliding,
minding my own business.
I felt free, free from worries
and I didn't care a thing
about anything, anyone.
Then!
Suddenly, the beauty
the freedom was broken ... nothing more.

Gradually the pupils began to extend this understanding of excellence, of grace. I think they began to find it even in human actions, in the way a pupil or a teacher or other adult reacted to a difficult situation – in a situation where there was a temptation to act blindly and bitterly. I think they began to see that a different response might be made not because they had been told that bitterness was wrong or sinful, or anything like that, but because they felt that generosity had a grace about it, the kind of excellence they had experienced in making a picture or singing a song. A whole new system of values began to emerge.

Quantity of information doesn't matter. In past generations many people with classical education have done excellent work in public affairs. The probability is that they would have done equally good work if they had been brought up as farmers or seamen or labourers, and there is much inquiry to be done into just what made them valuable people. Innate ability in the first place, probably (although that is not incontrovertibly proved, because a definition of general ability evaporates as you try to take hold of it and pin it down in words). But what were the things that gave some men a width of understanding, sympathy, made them hesitate to allocate blame and readily receive co-operation? Was it a background of rich example? People in their home or village who didn't grab, in the radiance of whose lives self-seeking and ambition seemed just a little vulgar, who remained good-humouredly in their place in the queue when other people elbowed and jostled their way to the front, people whose lives had an apparently effortless rounded excellence. Although they never, never preached, other people less sure of themselves seemed to be reproved by their inward peace. Now this is the kind of thing that we in the schools should be giving attention to.

We want to achieve not only individual excellence but a feeling of losing ourselves in a community. We in the Coal Town school have done this only at rare moments. At an end of term service on a golden July day the girls' choir sang a Bach anthem, *Bist du bei mir* and there was such a bell-like clarity of tone and desire to achieve excellence that some of us felt that this, appropriately at the end of the term, was a token of what we were trying to do.

Friendly visitors ask for evidence of success. 'Can you prove that this works?' We haven't much to offer in the way of evidence, and what we have is not easily measurable or even perceptible. The evidence many people seek is personal success and a realistic ability to conform to the facts of life (which means the demands of the establishment). I begin to see what is called indiscipline as evidence of a fearless spirit, and the pupils' resistance to our educational methods, even when it would pay them to accept, as evidence of integrity. I have learned to respect their disarmingly frank admission of the truth when a lie would have been easier. All we can do in the school is to help the pupils to develop those qualities of fearlessness and integrity with which they come to us already endowed. That, I think, is success.

The Spanish writer, Ortega y Gasset, published in 1930 a study of the phenomenon that has been occupying our attention in the Coal Town school. He called it *The Revolt of the Masses*. Athens and Rome, he said, never managed to make the masses feel that they were participating in the State, and therefore couldn't count on their patriotism but had to use exclusively bureaucratic measures of administration and warfare. Between 1800 and 1914 the population of Europe grew from 180 million to 460 million. In the nineteenth century they theoretically claimed the same rights as privileged people, but didn't really expect to exercise them; today, says Gasset, they *do* expect to exercise them. But they contributed, he claimed, none of the 'service to something transcendental that the élites contributed.' Because they had neither docility nor gratitude nor understanding, Gasset believed we were in for a difficult period of history – all the more difficult since today there are fewer cultured people, that is, people with a broad understanding of how 'society and the heart of man are to be organized.' Most scientists, said Gasset, behaved in almost all spheres of life as do the mass-men. There was a 'disarticulation of knowledge'.

There is a cold, haughty, Spanish hostility to the masses in Gasset's book. They now believe they are the State, he says, and they will more and more 'set its machinery working to crush beneath it any creative minority which disturbs it (in politics or in ideas or in industry).'

Now we in the Coal Town school knew from ten years' bitter experience what Gasset had in mind. We, too, tried to do some work which might be called creative and found the county council (a Labour council, alas!) setting its machinery working to crush beneath it our educational efforts. But we had the advantage of working thirty-seven years after the publication of *The Revolt of the Masses*, and we caught glimpses of developments that were invisible in Gasset's Europe.

He wrote, 'A people is capable of becoming a State in the degree to which it is able to imagine. Hence it is that with all peoples there has been a limit to their evolution in the direction of a State; precisely the limit set by nature to their imagination.' To that, we in the Coal Town would reply that there are indications (for the moment we wouldn't put it higher than that) that nature has set no limit to the imagination of the majority of people. What limits at present exist have been set by an élite's educational system, and the élite has not been at pains to see how imagination could be developed. It has been content to see it atrophy in our arid classrooms. V. S. Pritchett wrote: 'Our fossilized systems of education have concentrated on forming either a ruling or an obeying personality, and have sought to make both of these personalities superior to the creative individual.' The county council discourage creative work because this work has been discouraged in them also, and in so doing (as Gasset saw), they limit the degree to which our pupils will be able to participate in the State.

Gasset's analysis of civilization in 1930 led him by cold logic to make three striking prophecies. 'Before long there will be heard throughout the planet a formidable cry, rising like the howling of innumerable dogs to the stars asking for someone or something to take command, to impose an occupation, a duty.' The second was: 'We are at present about to assist, as in a laboratory, at a gigantic definitive experiment; we are going to see if England succeeds in maintaining in a sovereign unity of common life the different portions of her Empire, by furnishing them with an attractive programme of existence.' And the third prophecy was that Europe wouldn't be able to resist the 'gigantic human enterprise' of Bolshevism unless it also had a 'plan of a new life'.

The outlook is bleak. The prophets are uniformly pessimistic. At the end of his days an optimist like H. G. Wells came near to despair about the fate of Homo Sapiens. Orwell's forecast for 1984 was a nightmare. Orwell supplements Gasset. There will be, he says, no attractive programme of existence, no plan of a new life; so here is what will happen – in 1984. There is plenty of uncomfortable evidence to prevent us from dismissing Orwell's forecasts as merely ridiculous efforts to make our flesh creep. Jackson and Marsden's *Education and the Working Class* showed that new prefects of the establishment are being recruited from working-class children who have done better than others in gaining marks in examinations and have allowed their own roots to atrophy. Orwell foretold the emergence of rootless people, easily indoctrinated and highly accommodating to authority. Another symptom foretold by Orwell is defeatism, the feeling that there is nothing anybody can do to alter things; this defeatism exists now among able teachers who feel that we must bow down and make our peace with the examination system. A third symptom is the growing emphasis on bigness, especially big comprehensive schools. Mass-produced indoctrination is most efficiently carried out in large units. In these huge new schools the children from the secondary moderns, the 'Newsom children', will be an embarrassment, degraded like Orwell's 'proles'. Those of us who had imagined that the Labour Party would make fundamental changes in our society, and particularly in our educational system, now see their efforts overborne like an irrelevant eddy in a stream. There are indications that the Newsom children will fare worse in the comprehensive system, that Labour seeks only to replace one élite by another. The old pattern is emerging more clearly marked than before; Labour's educational system will impress these children more strongly than before with their insufficiency and, unless we reconsider the situation urgently, we shall be on our way to Ingsoc and 1984.

But a dazzling alternative presents itself. The Renaissance, which altered so much else, left education as it found it, the tool of governments. We are faced with the spectacular possibility that educational inquiry may be waking from its long sleep and, following the example of scientific inquiry, may declare its independence, its right to ask any questions whatsoever, no matter what their effect on principalities and powers. If that is so, one of the first questions will be, 'Is it a fact, or only a fiction necessary for the protection of an élite establishment, that the great majority of people are inferior to the élite and lack the ability to take an active part in government?' This implies the possibility of a society, totally new in history, in which everybody is regarded as a first-class citizen.

The fight for educational freedom of inquiry may be as fierce as was the fight for scientific freedom. Fundamental educational experiments may be resisted as fiercely as Galileo's, and for the same reason – an élite's fear of losing power. But if the free forces in education win, then 1984 will be averted.

Chapter Five
The Journeys

The naval base at Rosyth on the Firth offered to lend a two-storey barn at Loch Rannoch to any school that wanted to go in for the Duke of Edinburgh Award. The school accepted the offer and sent groups of boys for a week at a time to explore the Rannoch country. Then we thought we'd better get a place of our own, so as not to overtax the Navy's generosity, and we wrote to the Forestry Commission. They asked for fuller details of why we wanted a hut. We replied that we had in our care the fittest generation of Scotsmen and Scotswomen in history but that there was not sufficient provision to give them scope for their energies, and that a background of mountains might supply the needs that a background of pit bings failed to supply. The Forestry Commission wrote back offering to let us have a two-roomed cottage not far from the Navy's barn, set in the Black Wood of Rannoch, part of the ancient Caledonian Forest. The rent would be £1 a year. For two years we sent groups of ten pupils with a teacher for a week at a time to the hut.

The school set out suggestions for work to any teacher who would want to follow the suggestions, but if a teacher had ideas of his or her own about what should be done, it was left at that. In the school we wanted to find out how best to profit from these advantages. Some of the teachers were very good. Others found it heavy going. The least successful were those who had prepared a scheme of work and were determined to see it through. The most successful was a girl of twenty-one, an uncertificated teacher. When she and her group returned, I asked if she would write a report. She said reluctantly that she would. A few days later I said, 'What about this report?'

She replied, 'I've been thinking about it, but really we didn't do very much.'

'What did you do?'

'Sat around and talked, mostly. Sometimes we didn't even talk.'

'Were the girls difficult to get on with?'

'No. On the contrary, they were charming and co-operative.'

'Would they like to go back?'

'Yes, indeed. They were sad to leave Rannoch. One or two of them said that when the bus came to bring them back home, they would go and hide in the woods until it had gone.'

'Why did they like it there?'

'I don't know. People will say it was because of the Navy apprentices. Did you know they were in the barn down beside the loch when we were there?'

'Yes. But I didn't know in advance; otherwise we'd have sent a boy's party that week. Any difficulties?'

'Well, at first there were. Some of the girls would steal off to make a rendezvous with the Navy boys on the bridge over the Dall Burn. So I made an agreement with the girls. If they didn't go off without my knowledge I said we'd invite the boys up to the hut in the evenings. And we did. The girls baked and prepared tea for them and they came and sat and talked round the wood fire, and about ten I said wasn't it about time they were going back and they got up and said good night and there was no trouble. They were nice lads.'

'Anything else happened?'

'Nothing much. They liked going to the wee farm for milk in the mornings because they saw all the animals. They spoke to lots of people. It's such a different way of life from what they are accustomed to. That appealed to them.'

'This report?'

'Yes, I'll set down and gather together what we did and write a report. But, honest, it won't amount to very much.'

A day or two later she brought me the report, diffidently. When she'd gone I read it. The burden of education slipped away as I read, the failure, the criticism, the official obstruction seemed of little consequence in the presence of work of this distinction. This is the report:

Most of the children who came in this party were about fifteen years old and had never been farther north than Perth. The journey was therefore rather like a fairy-land trip for them. Lunch on Loch Tummel side was somewhat protracted since it was difficult to drag them away. Some of the children noticed that some of the trees were apparently growing under water and asked how this could happen. We then explained about the damming of the loch for the hydro-electric scheme and the subsequent water level rise. This was done briefly but it was raised again one evening by one of the children, so we discussed at length hydro-electric schemes, the grid system, the tremendous number of uses of electricity, the ruination of scenery by pylons and the flooding of some of the Welsh villages.

This was typical of all the teaching done at Rannoch. An observation, a comment and then, after the children had time to ponder on it, further discussion usually in the evening to leave the days free to observe. In this way, we covered forestry commission work, bracken prevention, soil erosion and forest clearance.

On one of our many expeditions, we noticed that one region of the forest seemed to have a great many dead trees and most of these looked as though they had been struck by lightning. This led to a multitude of questions. What was lightning, why did it strike things, what did it strike, where did it come from? Another example of this was the cuckoo. Returning from a trip into Kinloch Rannoch, we heard a cuckoo in a nearby wood. Not one child in the group had ever heard a cuckoo before. Many questions about the birds followed. Other birds then came into the discussion. A local child, who joined us at weekends, said she knew where some birds were sitting on nests. So we split into smaller groups and went off to see them. At first, the children had no idea how to move quietly and no patience to wait quietly, but by the end of the week they had become quite adept at bird-watching and one small group watched a lapwing patrolling the area round its nest and flying off as a decoy when disturbed, while its mate sat silent and motionless on the nest.

Local people took a great interest in the group and were exceedingly kind and helpful. The farmer who supplied the milk told them something of pasteurization, the gamekeeper told them about his dogs, their breed and training, what jobs they did, about deer on the hill, the stags losing their antlers. Mr Bayne, a retired estate worker, told them of the changes in the way of life in the last fifty years. The older people who lived and worked on the estate had had smallholdings. But now the smallholdings were all taken over by the Forestry Commission and the population was transient. The foresters and fellers moved on to leave the little huts for the bulldozer teams and then the planters. Mr Bayne was regarded as a bit of a wizard for his very accurate weather forecasts but he was very willing to impart the local signs of weather change, the mist on the hill, the clouds at the end of the loch, etc.

Plant, tree and bird identification were done on the spot and there are adequate reference books in the cottage for any child who is interested to pursue the matter further. Frogs abounded in the district and their life story was discussed. Insects, particularly ants, came in for a great deal of scrutiny and much of the children's aversion to 'creepy-crawlies' was lost as they discovered more about them.

Stray remarks sparked off discussion. As I was reading a newspaper I made a remark about Foster Dulles's illness. Who was Foster Dulles? What did he do? What was a Foreign Secretary? What did people in government offices do? A complete evening was spent discussing various items of news. The Notting Hill racial problem, the racial problems as seen in Little Rock and similar situations were discussed. Many of the children had little or no idea of recent events. The causes and background were talked about as long as time allowed. World Refugee Year came up. What were refugees? What were they fleeing from? Why did they have to flee? The British Commonwealth, the difference between colonies and self-governing members, all these were discussed in an informal fashion usually after supper. Newspapers became more than pieces of paper with cartoon strips and racing tips. Since our return to school many of the children have come to me and made some comment on an article or asked for an explanation of a situation.

In domestic matters, too, a large and varied field was covered. The children learned to work as a team and the importance of a routine in running a house. Rainwater was collected one afternoon and we had a general hair-washing night. The easy lather, the feel of the water and the general shining hair the next morning taught more vividly than any science lesson, the softness of water. As most of the girls were about to leave school and already wear make-up, we talked of hair care, personal hygiene and make-up for different type skins. The cooking was done completely by the children. We discussed the menus, with special reference to dietary requirements. They learned the value of certain mosses in keeping meat, milk, etc., cool, that cones gave a rapid heat and that some types of wood burn more quickly than others. The region is mainly coniferous so fires were apt to light easily but die down quickly, so they learned that a wood pile had to be kept stocked. Litter and sanitary disposal were dealt with, the children taking the rather unpleasant tasks in their stride. First aid in the home was being used regularly for minor cuts, bruises, etc.

The underlying atmosphere was learning when the occasion presented itself, when a bit of private thought had been done but without the 'glass-house forcing' that arises in a classroom. Time was the biggest enemy. Interest such as I had never seen in those children, was displayed over a variety of topics. Each one a topic which would have met with blank disinterest if introduced in the remote classroom but which blossomed in the informal atmosphere where no pressure to learn was applied.

Catharine Nimmo

This, I felt, was education at its best. The drudgery and ill-will were very far away from this luminous warmth, this quiet excellence.

Not all the pupils found the same enjoyment at Rannoch. I went up once and found a group of senior girls bored and difficult. We took them for a walk but they weren't interested in St Chad who lived in a cell at Rannoch and became Bishop of Lichfield; or Robert the Bruce who chased the English through a pass (still called 'The Glen of the Saxons'). I asked them:

'We've started these Rannoch visits and lots of people say they are a waste of time. Perhaps they're right. I don't think so. But I really don't know. None of you enjoyed this afternoon very much, did you?'

'No. There was too much walking.'

'Well, why do you like to be here?'

There was another pause. Then suddenly a girl spoke quickly, with venom. 'Well, at home they're nag-nag-nagging at you all the time. Do this and don't do that and hurry up, and so on it goes all the time. Never a minute's peace. They're at you in school and they're at you at home. But up here you get to do what you like and to do nothing if you feel like doing nothing.'

'Yes, that's right,' several voices echoed, as if the first girl had suddenly struck a chord to which they all vibrated. 'You get some peace up here,' another girl added.

Other reports brought back to the school told an unadorned story of children enjoying themselves. They dammed the burn and watched its level rise, canoed and swam in the loch, strung ropes across trees and climbed them. A teacher said that his group came equipped with cigarettes and he let them smoke; but when their supply was finished, they were so busy playing commandos in the woods that they didn't bother to buy cigarettes from the vans that called daily. They went every day for a barrowful of firewood from the sawmill, collected the milk, peeled the potatoes and did the other chores without fuss. 'What did they learn?' the traditionalist will ask, but that brings into debate the whole question of what 'learning' means. If it means memorizing information, the answer is probably not very much, although I'm not sure of that. They learned to adapt themselves to a simpler way of life and to find pleasure in simpler things. On getting up one summer morning a pupil said to me, 'Look how that birk (birch tree) shines in the sun.' Similarly I suppose the pupils find happiness in the dark shapes of trees against the moon, or the cosiness of the lamp-lit cottage and its quietness in the middle of the wood on a late autumn evening when the wind was blowing half-a-gale down at the loch, rustling through the dry leaves and making waves. I remember such an evening when the streamers of the Aurora Borealis were reflected in a pewter gleam on the surface of the loch as they shot up above a base of clouds along the summits of the mountains.

John Brown was due to attend the juvenile court for the third time, for stealing. It's a curious thing but you find there's usually at least one teacher who wants to put in a word for a pupil, however black the record against him seems to be, and one teacher said, 'You know, John Brown's not really a bad boy. Could we help him?' The likelihood was that John would be sent to an approved school, and, since he was already over fourteen, he wouldn't return to the Coal Town school. We decided to make a last attempt, but without much hope, to help him. A teacher on the staff, a skilful mountaineer, offered to take John and one of his pals, and two other boys whose reliability we knew, for a week's climbing at Glencoe. This was in January. They lived at the Glencoe Youth Hostel, where they had a warm and understanding welcome from the warden and his wife. The teacher explained the whole story to the warden, and the reason for the visit. The first day was spent in learning knots and practising on the lower slopes. Then they went to the higher mountains. They learned something of the historical background to the massacre in the valley nearly three hundred years ago, on a winter morning. They learned about living in the Highlands. They saw the wonder of a 'Brocken spectre', a reflection of themselves, gigantically magnified and within six concentric rainbows, on the clouds. They learned to depend on one another, four on a rope, cutting each step on frozen snow that gave way when they put pressure on it.

They met a blizzard on Argyll's highest mountain, Bidean, and some of them broke down and cried, out of fatigue and despair – and then went on; and arrived back at the hostel with a new confidence in themselves; and told two Liverpool climbers that Bidean is two hundred feet higher than Snowdon.

The social life in the hostel achieved as much as the climbing. Everything was open, and nothing stolen. One day the warden asked them if they knew anything about a window that had been broken. They said 'No' and the warden said, 'That's good'. Later, when they told the teacher about it, one of the boys said in surprise, 'And the warden believed us, sir.' It was a strange thing to see two sullen youths gradually, although suspiciously, re-entering society, exchanging the climbing stories of the day with an English vicar, taking part in the evening sing-songs. The other hostellers took an interest in the pupils and the pupils took an interest in the other hostellers. The first day John was on the mountain he said to the teacher, 'I wish I was dead'. On their last climb he said, 'I wish we could bide here all the time.' No doubt he was thinking partly of the juvenile court, two days ahead of him, and the music he would have to face there. But also I think he was thawing in the generous welcome of the Youth Hostel. When they got into the bus to leave, the warden's wife said, 'I hope you'll all come back soon. We've enjoyed having you.' And the astonished comment of one of the boys, some miles along the road was, 'Did you hear yon, sir? *And she meant it.*'

John attended the juvenile court on the day appointed. I think it says much for the Justices of the Peace that, on account of the school's report of John's achievement at Glencoe, he was given a further chance.

It was only later that we discovered that, on their last morning at Glencoe and while waiting for the bus to take them back to the Coal Town, John stole a ten-shilling note from a handbag lying on a table in the hostel common room. For this theft he had to attend another juvenile court, this time at Oban, and was sent to an Approved School.

There was enough money in the School Fund to send six pupils to Glencoe for a week, and another six the following week. We sent them off and the fortnight gave us time to raise some more money. A Friday night rock 'n' roll dance brought in another

£10. The BBC were approached and immediately commissioned a programme about the venture; the fee would help to finance further expeditions. A Glasgow business man sent a cheque for £25, and a member of the Colonial Service sent a cheque for £25. On neither of these men had the school any claim. An international trust, some business firms and an English youth club sent between them over £200. Pupils of an experimental primary school in Aberdeen collected and sent us £2 10s. All this generosity amazed the school, and our gratitude was mixed with the feeling that we had too easily under-estimated human beings. On the other hand, one pupil made 15s. selling coal he had collected from the bing, to help pay for his week at Glencoe.

And thus, throughout the year we managed to scrape the money together to keep pupils for a week in the mountains. Our pupils fought their way up Ben Nevis and the Cairngorms and An Teallach and across to Skye. They met blizzards and deluges. In Glen Etive in June they stumbled across a newly-born deer, the after-birth still attached to it. They watched golden eagles and came to recognize alpine flowers. Amongst remote hills they came on ruined clachans and their instructor explained to them why villages die. They dissected animals and talked to strangers and read books on mountaineering. The instructor was amazed at the physical endurance of these fourteen- and fifteen-year-old pupils. Strangers went out of their way to write to the school to praise the courtesy and consideration shown by the pupils. A group of girls went climbing, and captured the hearts of the Glencoe hostellers by their smiling grace and their excellent cooking. Pupils saved their money and bought tents and went off to the Highlands during the summer holidays. Back at the home base, the staff listened to the praise of their pupils with pleasure and pride but without surprise. We felt like saying, 'This is what we always said.'

Although the search for a shooting lodge in the Highlands grew out of the success of the small groups of ten pupils whom we sent to Rannoch for a week at a time, there was more to it than that. The failure of our orthodox methods of teaching in the Coal Town school was becoming more difficult to ignore, and we were realizing the futility of trying to sew temporary patches on an educational system that went on coming to pieces. We needed a place where we could make a fresh start from the foundations, where the pupils should have much greater freedom than the Coal Town school offered and where we could offer them a different curriculum. We felt that a large, old house in a remote part of the Highlands might be going cheap and we started to look for such a building.

We set out on the search gaily, like our own pupils on the first hours of a long, long hike. The sun was shining, we felt something of the elation of explorers who are sure of the value and success of their expedition. This was the kind of 'imaginative approach' to education that all the conference speakers recommended. There would be difficulties, of course, but they would be overcome. Eight years later I realize how little we appreciated the difficulties.

We wrote to the Forestry Commission, the Hydro-Electric Board, property agents in Edinburgh and private individuals, and we collected a list of buildings that were empty and might serve our purpose. It was a romantic list. We tracked down their position on the Ordnance Survey. To one of them we would have to bring stores by boat down a long loch. Another was on the fairy-like island which was said to be the scene of Barrie's play *Mary Rose*. A third was away at the other end of the Cairngorms. A fourth was in the Mamores. Another was remote in the Hebrides.

Some were far beyond our possible finances. Some were riddled by dry rot and beyond repair. We looked forward with expectation to each morning's mail wondering if any of these castles in the air could become the property of our pupils. Then one day a letter came from the British Aluminium Company asking further particulars of what we proposed to do with a shooting lodge. I replied at length, saying that we wanted to give our pupils scope, in exploring the Highlands and in forestry and in soil reclamation, for their abundant energies, peace to relax; and opportunities to learn about their country, its geology and natural history and economy, so that they could clearly understand and the more fully enter into their heritage. I believed that if they got away for a month at a time from the restricted life of the Coal Town and its classrooms, they might find a new confidence.

Then I was asked if I would go and look at Inverlair Lodge in

Lochaber and see if it was suitable for our school's purposes.

I found the house, a white three-storey building a mile off the Lochaber road near the head of Loch Treig. The front windows looked on to a deep bank of rhododendrons and a grass tennis court. At the side there was a large walled garden, but the garden had not been used for many years and rushes were growing there and in the tennis court. Beyond the rhododendrons, fields where sheep grazed sloped down to the River Spean and on the rise at the other side was the Loch Laggan to Fort William road and above it and parallel to it on the side of the mountain was one of the 'parallel roads' of which there are many in Lochaber. At the side of the house there was a little hill crowned by a small cairn commemorating the burial place of seven highlanders killed in an inter-clan feud.

We wandered through the house. It had been last occupied by commando troops seventeen years previously but it was surprisingly dry and in fairly good condition. Before that it had belonged to Lord Abinger. We tried to imagine his shooting parties in a pre-war August, a footman trimming the lamps, the housekeeper bringing out of a basket linen tablecloths as beautifully laundered as in a Dutch painting, scullery-maids chopping up carrots, a gardener with a basket of new potatoes and another of ripe peaches, everywhere the smell of venison coming from the ovens of the large kitchen range . . . and guests in leisurely ease at the other end of the house, sitting in the large room before a fire of peat and logs, discussing the day's bag and the morrow's weather and the glow of the heather in the corries.

Then we tried to imagine the house noisy with the chatter of the children of Fife miners, several groups of them just back from a long summer day in the hills, excitedly exchanging dramatic stories and humorous accounts of the day's adventures. They would talk of climbers they had met on the Polldubh Crags of Glen Nevis or on Sron na Garbh-bheinne, the Gaelic names tripping easily off their tongues as if they had never in their lives been within a hundred miles of a pit bing. In the spacious end-room they would be talking about an osprey they had glimpsed briefly in their binoculars, and spreading out for identification their day's trophies, a wasps' nest, a fox's skull, flakes of mica, alpine flowers, a handful of phosphorescent soil. A group would be recounting strange tales told them by a crofter in a remote glen. In the round room to the left of the main entrance one pupil would be already busy with paint brushes, trying from a pencil sketch in a notebook to make a picture of the Lost Valley, while the impression was still fresh in his memory; near him, on a chair another pupil busy with a knife carving a fantastic shape of tree-root into the likeness of an eagle.

One of the big rooms in the kitchen quarters would be a workshop. There would still be logs and peats for the fires, and the pupils would saw the logs and cut and dry the peats themselves. The two rooms in the servants' quarters which looked as if they had been dining rooms we would make into one large dining room and in winter evenings after the meal was cleared we would show films there. The large drawing room upstairs we'd convert into a library containing books of all kinds but with an excellent section on highland life and its history, fauna, flora and sports. In our noisy Coal Town there is little peace or accommodation for reading books, and we felt that the long stretch of time after the winter sun had gone down behind the snows of Cruach Innse would encourage pupils, initially hostile to books, to stroll round the library and see what it had to offer and finally to settle in comfort with a book before the library fire.

The house was divided into two quite separate parts for servants and guests and, except on the ground floors, these two halves were completely blocked off from one another. This division would fit in easily with our plan for boys' and girls' dormitories, and we would provide the separate accommodation and baths to meet the requirements of the Education Department.

Near the cool room where the butler stored his wines, there was a small room which had a grating over the window and an electric light stuck horizontally into a fitting behind an iron grating above the door. The door itself was strong and in the top half a small pane of glass covered by a sliding shutter. It was obviously a prison, and for a prisoner that the warders were taking no chances with. The employee of British Aluminium who was showing us round explained, 'That's where Rudolf Hess was held during the war.'

The making of aluminium needs a tremendous amount of electricity, and that was available in Lochaber in the form of waterpower. In order to get water, British Aluminium had to buy large stretches of land, with the houses, and Inverlair was one of those houses. The water supply from Spey and Laggan flows near Inverlair on its way to make aluminium and now paper. From the front windows of Inverlair you can see the railway which takes trees to be made into chips for pulp at Fort William. We should like to supply our pupils with paper made out of that water and those trees. We want them to see at first hand the web of economic life, the interdependence of foresters and lockkeepers and railwaymen and electricians and papermakers and printers and the people who provide them with entertainment, build houses for them, feed them.

I wrote to British Aluminium and asked them how much they would sell the house for. They said they had been taken over by an American firm and there might be more delay than there would otherwise have been, but that in the meantime they would get valuers to work out a price. We waited with barely concealed impatience, eager to get cracking on the job of transforming a shooting lodge into a school. The staff discussed plans. We estimated that it would cost us £2 10s. to keep one pupil there for a week, and thought that if we could get parents to pay 15s. of that, weekly, the County Council might subsidize them to the extent of the remaining £1 15s. From the parents' point of view, the fifteen shillings wouldn't stop any pupil from going to the Highlands, since a pupil, we estimated, would eat food to that value at home. From the County Council's point of view we felt that, since educationists were clamouring for more experimental work to be done, they would not be against financing a pilot experiment of this kind for a period of (say) three years. We asked for tenders for rewiring the house and for dealing with the plumbing. The rest of the work of converting the house would, the technical staff said, be done by the pupils under their direction. Small groups would go up, as soon as permission had been got from the Education Committee, and spend part of their time in the mountains, and the rest working in the house, preparing it for fuller occupation. For these groups, life would at first be austere. They would have to cook their own food on primus

stoves. But they would sleep softly enough because a year previously it had been discovered that a Fife shipbreaking firm was
selling single beds, substantially made of oak, and mattresses,
for £2, and £40 of the School Fund's small resources was in-
vested in buying twenty of these beds against the day when we
would have a highland home of our own. These beds were stored
in the school, ready to move up when we got the green light. So
with high hopes we wrote to the Education Committee asking if
they would support the scheme, make us an initial grant of £2500
(to pay plumbers, electricians and for the materials our pupils
would use) and an annual sum of £2500, most of which would
be required to subsidize the pupils, thirty of them for a month
at a time, during their visit to Inverlair.

Concurrently with instruction in mountaineering and sailing,
we wanted to create a cultural background which would really
nourish our pupils. A word like 'cultural' is vague and suspect,
but we were clear enough in our own minds what we were after.
We wanted to show our pupils the marks torn by the claws of
the glaciers on the high rocks and left to show their power. We
wanted them to stand on the parallel road and visualize the glen
when it was a deep loch whose level was above the present house.
We wanted them to visit the green outposts of Christianity north
of Rannoch and deep in Glen Roy dating from the first millen-
nium when lonely men in remote cells talked about a different
way of spending your time. We would take them on the forced
marches and hurried journeys through these same hills made by
Montrose and Claverhouse to impose by force their own interpretations of this teaching. We would take them over the drove
roads and tell them the story of the poverty and the romance,
the straight-dealing and the cattle-rustling of the days when the
main product of the Highlands was cattle. We would take them
over Wade's tracks and the patrol routes of the Redcoats after
the 'Forty-five rebellion and let some of the gas out of the gay
balloon of the Jacobites and the eagle-feathered Highland chiefs,
and explain the romance of the incredible achievement of Telford,
opening up the Highlands, bringing a better life. We would tell
them of the humour of the building of the Caledonian Canal, and
the inordinate amount of porridge eaten and whisky drunk by
the navvies.

We would tell them about the Highland clearances and take them on journeys to the clachans that were cleared, so that the scattered stones of these ruins should speak to them. We would tell them about animal and plant life, and the untapped economic wealth of the region. They would work at forestry and farming and take part in the land-reclamation that is going on near Inverlair, and in the evenings study the background to these things, botany and soil chemistry and economics, and keep themselves in food from the school garden and keep the house in repair.

Occasionally members of the school staff would escape from the Coal Town to visit Inverlair and they would come back with new ideas to discuss and work out in detail so that we should be ready to put them into practice when the time came.

'We must think big,' the principal art teacher said, and that is what the teachers were doing. They would teach the pupils fly-fishing, and tell them the life histories of the flies that fish leap out of the water to devour on summer evenings. They would look for gnarled pieces of strangely shaped tree roots preserved in the peaty soil and carve them. They would carve deer antlers in the long winter evenings. They would revive the making of coracles and try to sail them. A deer stalker said he would take the pupils, one or two at a time, with him, and from him they would learn about deer. They would skate on a frozen loch and learn the ancient game of curling. There would be a relaxed atmosphere in which alone nourishing discussion and creative work take place. This was one of the things that caught the enthusiasm of the teachers, the feeling of peace about the place. (Maybe this is what we're all looking for.) They would paint pictures. In that peace the pupils develop a fuller awareness of their surroundings. A teacher told me that a group of pupils at Rannoch had told her that they had seen thirty-two different shades of green round about the loch and in the woods in late spring.

The teachers spoke with an immensely captivating and an almost naïve enthusiasm of the things they would do when we finally moved into Inverlair. I realized that this would be a success because it would be a communal effort. It had captured the enthusiasm of so many adults.

These foundations having been laid, we sat down and waited

for our castle in the air to float to the earth and settle solidly upon them.

But a dream is an intractable thing when you come to tie it down, and more difficult to transmute into reality than we had expected. We were inundated with reasons, given by members of the Education Committee, for not going ahead with the scheme. This was not real education. We would be better advised to stick to our job of putting the three Rs into the pupils instead of this nonsense of taking them gallivanting over the hills. There were too many frills in education nowadays, wasting the tax-payers' money. One member referred to the weekly newspaper which the school published and said that this was the kind of thing we were up to and that Inverlair was just another example of it. One diehard said the scheme would have been all very well if it were limited to the élite of pupils in the High Schools, but he wouldn't support the granting of this money for the use of Junior Secondary pupils. We were asked if we would be prepared to share the house with the other schools of the county, letting each of them have it for a fortnight. The answer to that was no. Good although it would have been to send some pupils from a large number of schools to the Highlands for a fortnight throughout the year, we were aiming at something much farther-reaching than Outward-bound courses. We were aiming at a remodelling of an educational system.

Months passed and the proposal limped through committee after committee. First the Schools Sub-Committee considered it on principle and then the Education Committee itself considered it on principle. Then the Schools Sub-Committee considered the question of supporting it financially. Then the Education Committee considered it financially.

The councillors' objections to the scheme were many. One said that schools should stick to normal work. Another said that they wouldn't dream of sending their pupils to such an old house. Another said that our plan to get a technical teacher and a team of older boys to repair woodwork would be resisted by the Trade Unions. (Although in fact the Trade Unions never did express disagreement.) Another said that this use of 'child labour' would put carpenters in the Highlands out of a job.

Another objection was that there was some doubt if a school

could be legally permitted to own a property like Inverlair, a point on which the lawyers disagreed, and we were told that the wording of the law was so indefinite that it might take a test case to establish whether we were legally entitled to go ahead.

On the other hand the members of the Education Committee were honest, well-intentioned men, making the best decisions, according to their lights, that they could. It was not the Committee's fault that they had been brought up in a rigid traditional system of education which discouraged imagination or change. The County Council was by a small majority a Labour Council, but some of the members who wanted to change the political system were keenest in opposing changes in the educational system.

Two things must be said in fairness to the Committee. They had a better record than most Scottish counties for generosity in educational expenditure. And about half of them supported the Inverlair's scheme, some of them defending it in spite of bitter attacks from colleagues of their own party.

On the eve of the Christmas holidays, five months after I had first visited the house, there was a sudden development. A letter came from British Aluminium saying that their board in London had discussed the proposal and agreed to offer the house to us as a present for the educational purposes we had described. I made the surprise announcement during the school's Christmas party and it brought elation to the pupils. They had become the owners of a shooting lodge in the Highlands. No longer were we faced with the task of raising the purchase price of the house; we looked forward to speedy progress.

But month followed month, meeting followed meeting, and little progress was recorded. At length, in June, an imposing group of local government conveners and officials visited Inverlair. There were the County Convener, the Finance Convener, the Convener and Vice-Convener of the Education Committee, other Councillors, the County Clerk, the Director of Education, the County Architect and the County Treasurer. They walked quickly through the building, decided that it was 'dilapidated', ordered the school to send no pupils to the house until it had been repaired by tradesmen and asked the architect to prepare a plan for altering the house to make it suitable for the use to which we proposed to put it.

The architect, I was afterwards told, found this a difficult assignment. He asked for a ruling about the standard of accommodation to which the building should adhere. The Committee left it to his judgement and he had to decide whether he would go for Youth Hostel conditions or boarding school conditions. His department carefully collected information about both types and a group from his office visited Inverlair. Architects prepared plans. We were invited to look at them. They were admirable. Skill and imagination had been brought to create a dream house, worthy of its incomparable surroundings. For half an hour we forgot our troubles and abandoned ourselves to the dream that was defined in firm lines on an official plan. Interior walls had been knocked down, and I imagined the mountaineers on a late winter's afternoon opening the front door and stepping into a large hall where flickering shadows from a huge wooden fire were dancing on the pastel-coloured walls. This was a beautiful creation, comfortable with all modern conveniences. How the pupils would love it! What a difference it would make to them to live among the mountains all day and be surrounded by this grace of living in the evening! And then, having briefly wallowed in the sunshine of this dream house, we stepped out into cold reality. The price? £22,000. We knew, of course, that the Finance Committee would never sanction such an expenditure.

And that was what happened. The whole plan was turned down on account of expense. The cost of the making of the plan together with estimated fees for the Clerk of Works was about £2000 – the sum we estimated would be required to make the house habitable.

We tried to explain to the Committee that we had never asked for this standard of accommodation and that in fact we didn't want everything to be laid on for our pupils. We said that we wanted to make the restoration of the building part of their technical education. We wanted them to take over the building themselves and improve it gradually, so that they felt it was their building, that *they* had made it and had a stake in it. We suggested that this was a more realistic kind of technical education than making a poker or a pipe rack for your grandfather. We didn't want a five-star hotel. Neither we nor in fact the pupils had the slightest objection to austere conditions. All we wanted were the bare requirements necessary for health. We hoped gradually, as we raised money and as the pupils suggested ideas, to improve the building and add extra comforts.

I wrote to the Carnegie UK Trust and suggested that Andrew Carnegie, who had been born and brought up less than a score of miles from the Coal Town, had left money to encourage experimental work of this nature and that the education of the sons of Fife miners would have appealed to him, but the Trust replied (reasonably enough) that they could hardly finance an educational experiment that hadn't received the support of the local Education Committee. The Trustees of Ford, Gulbenkian and Nuffield similarly returned a polite 'No' to our pleas. Another Christmas arrived; a year had elapsed since British Aluminium presented us with the house, and we were no further forward. The proposal was still bogged down amongst the committees.

Fortunately they had not turned the proposal down absolutely. A compromise was suggested, which was that I should take steps to bring the house up to the standards of accommodation reached by the Camp Schools.

We had thus reached the situation that we had to carry out renovations in the house but we couldn't use the help of the pupils since we were prohibited from taking them into the house until the renovations were completed. We would therefore have to employ workmen. But the committee wouldn't grant us any money to do that, nor would they declare that they supported the scheme so that the Carnegie UK Trust should be able to give us money.

At this time, too, the principal technical teacher came along and said that the school bus, which the pupils had saved up to buy five years previously, needed two new tyes and that it would be dangerous to send pupils out in it until it had been re-shod. We had no money in the school fund, and I asked the Committee if they would allow me to take the price of two new tyres out of the £2000 which they allowed us annually for text-books and equipment. I described the value of the bus to the pupils. It took them for swimming lessons to a pool which a linoleum factory, twenty miles distant, allowed us to use. It took them to the Highlands for camping and trekking. It took them on visits to factories and exhibitions in Glasgow and Edinburgh, at a small fraction of what public transport would have cost. But the committee wouldn't allow us to take the price of two tyres out of our annual allocation, and we had to take the school bus off the road. The restriction in the scope of the pupils' activities was felt too keenly; the technical department sold two of the canoes which the pupils had made in order to buy the two tyres, and the bus was on the road again.

It seemed incredible to us that the County Council should insist that pupils remain in the ugly Coal Town classrooms when Inverlair opened such opportunities. One autumn day when I was travelling by train to Inverness the council's attitude seemed more than usually beyond understanding. Even on an autumn day the Highlands shone and dazzled in the clear air, as clear as the South African sunshine. Only when a wind blew air high over the top of a hill was it turning into cloud. Loch Ericht snaked out of sight to the west of the train, luring your thoughts Rannochwards. At Dalwhinnie the grey-granite bright road over the hill towards Laggan and Inverlair shone clearly. The oaks were brown like cinnamon and the birches, higher up the mountain slopes and now leafless, had streaks of silver running down their bark. To the east were the Cairngorms, their skylines very clearly defined. The Highlands were ablaze with colour. The rowans were scarlet. Leaves just beginning to fade were coloured lemon and orange. Larches, changing colour, were a soft muffled greeny-brown. There was a maple tree, a red glory singing in the sunshine. Clear burns were tumbling down in a hurry, their stones and pebbles clearly seen. The background was the face of the mountains corrugated with wrinkles. In the midst of this autumn colouring, the vivid green of broom made a contrast. The waters were racing along. The sky was clear blue.

I thought of the pupils at their council meeting the previous day, discussing lesbianism in the Coal Town, and pupils in Coal Towns all over the country, bending their heads over classroom textbooks; and it seemed to me clearer than ever before that our schools are in the Middle Ages. The Cambridge Modern History speaks of a monk walking along the shores of Lac Leman, pulling his cowl closer over his eyes in case he should be lured from his thoughts of heaven by the beauty of the earthly lake. The Education

Authorities of the twentieth century have much in common with the medieval religious authorities.

The staff discovered that at Grantown-on-Spey was the only school in Scotland which made its own skis, and off they went to visit Grantown-on-Spey to learn about it. They found seasoned ash in a local sawmiller's yard and bought it. A Heath Robinson-like steamer was set up in the woodwork room to bend the ash, and it worked. The winter was a particularly hard one and even the hills of Fife offered ski runs; so some of the teachers took pupils at week-ends to try out the new homemade skis and learn to make a herring-bone pattern on the snows of the Lomonds and Largo Law. Then farther afield to the steeper Highland slopes.

After that they started making lobster creels, and pupils went out and set them at night and got up early in the morning to inspect the catch. More boats were being made. And although we didn't have the money to continue with the previous year's gliding, the staff made a wind tunnel and worked at models to demonstrate the theory of flight, in the hope that later we might resume our weekly gliding instruction beside Loch Leven. The warmer weather came and groups studied the inter-tidal life along the shore and reported on the new birds and plants as they appeared in Keil's Den, the valley where Robinson Crusoe used to wander alone after his return from his desert island. We worked away steadily, looking forward all the time to the much wider scope that Inverlair offered.

Permission to stay on Rhum is granted only to scientists, naturalists and qualified mountaineers. The pupils felt highly privileged to live on the island for a fortnight.

On a May morning we left the Coal Town in the school's minibus. By evening we were looking down on Loch nan Uamh on the west coast where Prince Charles's boat brought him from France in 1745. Near here we pitched our tents for the night.

Next morning we came up by Arisaig to Mallaig. There was a soft air and little showers of rain came on and gave way to sunshine and I suppose that is why the broom glowed so richly yellow. The blackthorn was out. There's an inexplicably plaintive feeling about Mallaig that I find it difficult to shake off, as if it were in tune with the Gaelic song that Wordsworth described in *The Solitary Reaper*.

Not all the busy port activity can dispel this atmosphere. A diesel engine was panting in Mallaig Station and people were queuing for the morning papers in the middle of the forenoon. Big white MacBrayne passenger boats swung into the harbour. Cranes were busy loading. Mallaig has the air of a frontier, where you prepare to enter a different world. There was a motor van to be hoisted aboard for the Outer Hebrides, Esso for Canna, bottles of methylated spirits, meat and sausages for Rhum, mailbags, rucksacks, newspapers, a plastic rubbish bin, all the extras from the modern world that help to make living in remote places more comfortable. The pupils piled their kit on the wharf and climbed down to the fishing boats to talk to the fishermen. Hamish Brown and I went to park the school's bus at the back of a hotel and drink coffee, looking out over the sea towards the islands. When we got down to the harbour again, we found the pupils laden with freshly caught fish which the fishermen had presented them with after hearing their story. Then the pupils spread through the town until it was time to return again to load our kit on to the smaller boat that was leaving for the islands at half past one. Later we heard about an incident that took place in a little crowded shop. A pupil had stolen postcards and a sheath knife and was showing them to his pals. One of them said, 'Ach, ye dinna dae that here. They're *nice* folk.' The boy replaced the goods he had taken.

The boat made its way out into the Sound of Sleat and the pupils looked at Scotland from the sea for the first time, the ground rising in knobbly hills behind Mallaig. They ate slices of bread and jam. In an hour and a half we were off the island of Eigg and waited for the boat to come alongside.

The next stop was off the island of Muck. While we waited for the Muck boat to come out, a woman who was going to go ashore in it told me about the island. 'There's a wee school', she said, 'and a young schoolmistress who comes from Bridgwater in Somerset.'

'How did she come to take a job in Muck?'

'She came for a holiday once and liked it and when there was a vacancy for a schoolteacher she applied and got it.'

By this time the boat had cleared the lee of the island and was tossing about in fairly heavy seas. There were two boatmen and a girl aboard.

'That's her.'

A girl in her twenties was standing at the stern of the boat, moving with its pitching as if she'd spent all her life sailing between Hebridean islands. When they came alongside I shouted to her above the wind, 'I'm in the same trade as you are. How do you like it here?'

She laughed. 'I love it.' She obviously did.

The passenger climbed aboard the small boat and away it went. We turned to starboard north west between Muck and Eigg. The pupils watched the receding outline of Muck and searched the horizon for the hills of the Ardnamurchan peninsula. Then (with binoculars) they looked at the shearwaters flying low over the sea. The three islands share one doctor and he had come on board to go and visit a patient, and told us about the difficulties of meeting urgent calls on islands separated by miles of sometimes stormy seas, but he too, like the Somerset girl, had found that the advantages of a remote life outweighed the discomforts.

In the late afternoon we sailed into Loch Scresort which is like a niche cut out of the east coast of Rhum. Piles of rucksacks and food boxes were lowered on to the boat that came out to meet us. We landed at the jetty and went to look for a camping site. We found it on soft level ground amongst trees on the south shore of the bay. The pupils, old hands at the game, set up their tents, got out their primus stoves, peeled potatoes. They cooked in small groups, supping their soup while the potatoes boiled. Then there was the sizzling of sausages, the sound of knives and forks on enamel plates, loud Fife voices raised in jokes, strangely incongruous in the midst of the peace of a larch wood above a Hebridean bay. From the water came the sound of eider ducks. 'Listen to them', Hamish Brown told the pupils. 'I always think they make a sound that reminds you of old ladies when they are shocked. Listen!' And indeed it was just like that. 'Oh, Oh! . . . Oh, Oh!'

The pupils finished their sausages, potatoes and peas, tinned fruit, tea and cake. Then they washed up, a trifle unwillingly, and went to explore their surroundings. The light was ebbing away when they struggled into their sleeping bags and closed the tent flaps and fell asleep to the sound of eider ducks uttering their pained, shocked exclamations.

Next morning we divided into two parties and went on a leisurely exploration of the island. It was a beautiful warm May day. We passed the cluster of houses and the post office at the head of the bay and took a road to the north. There was novelty at every turn of the road. Those of us who live in the Scottish industrial belt generally know little of the Highlands and less of the Western Islands. There they have a different language and a different way of life. It is a foreign country as new and strange to a Fifer as Andorra or Lichtenstein. The people of the west have some strange beliefs incomprehensible to a Lowlander. They sometimes seem to believe in fairies and second sight; they don't believe in hard work. Not that the Lowlanders are all that enthusiastic about hard work; but they regard it as unavoidable, part of the scheme of things. The Highlanders have escaped this indoctrination; they have a quiet and easy philosophy of their own.

We strolled along the wide Kinloch Glen, slaking our thirst from time to time in an ice-cold burn. Then a zoologist in a Land Rover stopped and we piled in and he ran us three miles north through the terminal moraines of Kilmory Glen till we reached the north coast at Kilmory. From the wonderful silver sands we bathed and came near to an inquisitive seal swimming inshore. Then I strolled along the east shore of the bay and looking over the western shoulder of Rhum saw, close at hand, the islands of Canna and Sanday. When I look back on it now I remember it as one of the most peaceful, happy days in my life. There were just the sea and the sky and the islands, and the much-contorted red rock enclosing the sands, and the inquisitive seal. No pressures. We wandered back to where the zoologist had left his Land Rover. Through his telescope he was studying deer, picking out the numbers on metal ear tags at a hundred yards. The Nature Conservancy was carrying out research on deer in the enclosed area of the island, he told us. In order to keep them from multiplying beyond the food resources of the island, they shot the stags. The venison is exported to Germany, and, he suggested, returns to us as Frankfurter sausages.

At the edge of the bay was a small building that housed a laundry, now no longer used. But in Victorian times the proprietor of Kinloch Castle on Loch Scresort sent his washing five miles across the island by pony trap so that there should be no washing of dirty linen in public.

Then the zoologist offered to take us on an eight mile run to the south-west of the island. In a cave we saw wild goats and their kids. The goats were long haired and shaggy like Highland cattle but had white tails. There were 'lazy beds' into which long ago crofters had scraped the thin soil, economizing on it to provide sufficient depth of soil for their crops. The golden voice of the cuckoo and the twittering of sandpipers ('diddit-dah dah-dit' like morse code) mixed with the sounds of Manx shear-waters, guillemots and cormorants. The ruins of the crofts remained, walls four feet high made of round sea-worn stones, dividing their homes into rooms seven feet square, and a big field, twenty-seven yards by thirteen yards, walled round. In these quiet places you feel the presence of the past or rather you feel that it was only the day before yesterday that our forebears put those stones together to make houses.

The Aberdeen zoologist was the perfect teacher. He talked to us as we bumped over the narrow road, and things that we would not have noticed came into the focus of attention and gained human significance. Those stretches of broom and furze were intended to fix nitrogen in the soil. See that dam over there? We'll go across and have a closer look at it. It was built to create enough depth of water to encourage sea-trout to go upstream. But the men who planned it under-estimated the power of a Rhum burn in spate and it caved in. In places like Rhum you become more intimately aware of the background of the stage on which man plays his part, the natural forces which he seeks to overcome and which hem him in. Gravity pulls down the walls of his houses; water power breaks the dams and perhaps his spirit; and he starts optimistically on some other temporary ploy until his tenure is up.

In the evening after supper I came on Hamish Brown and some pupils whom he had taken for a stroll along the coast. They strolled along leisurely, now watching a merganser on Loch Scresort through the binoculars, now looking for an invisible snipe, the drumming of whose wings we heard as it moved in circles overhead. We came upon a ruined clachan, solidly built of sea-rounded stones. It had been inhabited perhaps a hundred and fifty years ago by crofters driven from the Isle of Skye, and when this settlement also had to be given up, it is likely that many of them went to America like so many other good Europeans. Otters had taken over this desolate clachan in Rhum and made of it a centre. It was criss-crossed by their runs and littered with shellfish shells. Pieces of spraint lay here and there and in one piece we found a length of nylon which had survived unaffected the influence of the otter's digestive juices. The Highlands and Islands are full of clachans that have died. I don't know how much the pupils would take out of this discovery. Maybe one day they'll sit down and figure out the things that belong to their peace, and how much the peace and quiet of a life lived looking out on the Sound of Sleat would weigh in the balance against greater financial rewards in an industrial area.

Next day the Nature Conservancy Warden took us up to the mountains. At about 2000 feet well up the side of Hallival, we sat down to eat our sandwiches while he told us about Manx shearwaters. As he spoke we gazed at the amazing view, all the way from the neighbouring island of Canna across the Minch to the mountains of Uist in the Outer Hebrides. No lecturer ever had a more wonderful stage. Far below and all round lay the sea, and pieces of land here and there like ornaments in a water bowl. The sun shone very warm even at that height. All round us grew richly green grass.

'It's manured by the shearwaters' droppings and mulched by their scratchings,' said the Warden. 'The parent birds return to the same nest year after year, but the young finds its own way to the sea somehow or other, and never returns to its home nest.'

Although the shearwaters are webbed-footed sea birds their nests are near the mountain tops, he said. They make burrows like rabbits and lay the eggs at the end of the burrow. 'And,' he said, removing a disc of turf and a stone close to where he sat, and pushing his arm down the space into the soil, 'here is a shearwater.' In his hand as by magic he held a sooty black bird the size of a pigeon. Its underside was white and the tip of its beak was bent like a tin opener. 'And this,' he added, plunging his arm again into the hole, 'is the shearwater's egg.' It was indistinguishable from a domestic hen's egg.

The pupils followed the Warden doing his round of the nests, removing a disc of turf, a stone underneath, a shearwater and its egg, and replacing them in reverse order, sometimes ringing one of the birds, and removing for chemical examination any egg that the shearwater had pushed out towards the entry of the tunnel. He told them about a fall of rock that had made some birds homeless. They came out at night to feed and couldn't get back in and didn't know what to do.

We studied the seascape and compared it with our Ordnance Survey map and began to find clues that hitherto had escaped us. A few names were in English, such as Schooner Point and Loch Mitchell; and the digging up of that history might be a ploy for another day; but the great majority were in Gaelic – Sgor Mhor, Rubha Port na Caranean. But the names of most of the highest mountains were in Scandinavian. It wasn't difficult to deduce that the Vikings, roving south-westwards by Shetland and Orkney and the north coast of Scotland and the Minch, and searching the horizon for landmarks, had given their own names to the highest mountains – Barkeval, Hallival, Askival, Trollaval. The Warden spoke of the trolls – gnomes, friendly but mischievous supernatural figures that the Scandinavians believe in – and the pupils started to put their pieces of new knowledge together. Why should the Vikings call that mountain just a mile to the south-west of Hallival where we stood, the Mountain of the Trolls? The Warden said that trolls meant 'the voices that make a sound in the night'. We could imagine Viking crews, about to fall asleep on the planks of their high-beaked rowing boats or in a sheltered creek, hearing inexplicable mutterings in a May night coming from the mountain tops, and nodding their heads to one another and saying, 'The Trolls!'

We climbed on through the craggier part to the summit of Hallival. Some of the pupils found and identified lady's alpine mantle, purple saxifrage and mountain sorrel. At the top it was warm and the view was magnificent, a vast extent of calm blue sea ringed by islands, the Outer Hebrides, Skye (two gems of snow shining in recesses of the Cuillins), Soay (from which Gavin Maxwell conducted his shark-fishing enterprise), the white sands of Morar, Eigg and Muck. Over in the direction of Trollaval a cuckoo was shouting. Then out of the calm we saw a change of weather coming in from over the Atlantic, approaching Scotland almost like a flotilla at ten knots, gathering cloud and roughing the sea's surface.

Here and there on the mountains were brown sandy flats where grass grew and there were nooks full of primroses overlooking precipitous burns.

Hamish Brown came to see me off on the Saturday morning boat. The pupils didn't bother getting up. Perhaps that noisy cuckoo that I'd heard close at hand at 2 a.m. had kept them awake. They had another week on the island. Once in Glencoe a Coal Town boy had told me, 'I wish I could bide here.' I felt the same as we came along the precipitous eastern coast of Eigg. The brown columns of basalt were like a huge crude Alhambra and through the glasses I could see clearly an eagle standing-atop these battlements. We put into the little jetty of Eigg and then crossed towards the mainland. The skipper brought us each a mug of tea. I felt a childish satisfaction in stretching the wings of my newly gained knowledge and identifying guillemots and lesser black-backed gulls and differentiating between adult and immature herring gulls and seeing the yellow flash on the head of a gannet; and at a considerable distance identifying shearwaters from their flight – first propelling themselves by their wings and then gliding freely, rather like a boy pedalling furiously on a bicycle so that he could the longer enjoy a spell of free wheeling.

If groups of monkeys are overcrowded, says an Oxford biologist there are brutal dictatorships and constant outbreaks of violence. We have found that the same is true of adolescent children in a Fife mining community. When we have taken these same children into the spaciousness of the country-side even for a week at a time, the destruction, the boredom and the cruelty have largely disappeared. Temporarily.

Many members of the staff gave up free time to supervise rock 'n' roll dances to raise pennies to help finance these trips, but even so it was only those pupils who could pay £2 10s. who could go for a week's journey. Parents came to tell us about the difference in attitude that even one week at Rannoch had made in a boy. Occasionally difficult children were referred to us by the psychiatrists so that they could benefit from a week in the open air far from the Coal Town.

Sometimes I went out with pupils on these journeys, ostensibly to keep in touch with what was happening, but really to escape with them from routine. It was wonderfully refreshing. Perth is a lowland town, but a few miles north the Highlands begin. There is a small loch where coot and swans swim close to the main Perth-Inverness road and that loch is at the gateway to the Highlands. Beyond it you already begin to breathe an ampler air, a slower rhythm takes over. Back in the Coal Town, trees, flowers, sky don't come much into the picture; here they are in the foreground and we become part of the march of the seasons across the landscape. In the Coal Town the events noticed and recounted concern people, their good or ill fortunes; here the last snow, the first primrose are also events, news.

The days of escape to the hills remain in clear detail in the memory. At Dalnaspidal on the last Sunday of June a man was washing his clothes in a hill burn. We had breakfast on the grass beside the railway line and at eleven set off south-west along Loch Garry. Often on the main road passing Dalnaspidal I'd caught a glimpse of the loch luring the eye and the imagination into the wild hinterland and I'd say that one day I'd go and see what it was like. The youngsters found novelties at every few yards – a deer antler, a deer skull, a lump of quartz, sheep wool, cotton grass, the blue flower of insectivorous butterworts, a dragonfly flitting about like a helicopter. On the loch side there was a building, housing a wire netting framework which could be let down to the bed of the loch by the unwinding of wire ropes wound round wheels, and we tried to deduce its function. Nearby was a larger building with a deep well which went down to the water of the Garry tunnel, part of the hydro-electric system. Beside us was a scatter of glacial moraines, like gigantic molehills, and we tried to re-create the situation in which they were deposited. There were parallel roads recording the margins of the loch when it stood at a level half-way up the mountainside and we compared these eroded margins with the similarly formed level stretches on the sandy shores of the loch which indicated the different levels at which the water had stood during the past year. When the road gave out, we walked through marshy ground, disturbing grouse, partridges, peewits and curlews. We found many chicks and one grouse nest and four eggs.

We came to a very large sheepfold on solid grassy ground and then an empty house. Again we could imagine the work that the generations who had lived in the house had accomplished – the stone-built sheepfold, the straight ditches (now overgrown) to drain the water, the grassy fields where the heather was now re-appearing on the hillside and which were reverting to bogland on the level ground. But it was encouraging to find that recent and much deeper ditches had been mechanically excavated in the bog-land. Modern man had come to take up the fight that the crofters had carried on against odds to colonize and make habitable this part of the country. I found it strangely comforting, exhilarating even, and I'm sure the old crofters would have felt happiness in seeing a rejuvenescence of their work, a feeling that man hadn't given up the struggle for an existence in the Highlands.

Here and there in the squelchy earth we came on old tree roots. 'Trees grew here once,' I said. 'There may be trees again,' said a thirteen year old pupil.

In these lonely places, children are responsive to atmosphere. Once, in the Corrieyairack, after a cloudy spell the sun came out and one of them said it *felt* warmer and added, 'I don't mean warm, but comfortable. You feel happier.' I shared this feeling. Living out of doors you feel dependent on the moods of the weather and even your spirits are subject to its whims.

Not all our journeys were successful. One of the trips had repercussions. Over forty pupils took the bus to Anstruther and climbed aboard the *Mona Lisa*, a fishing boat which had been converted to take trippers to the Isle of May in the Forth. The island is a nature reserve, the home of seabirds, and measures over a mile long and a quarter of a mile wide. We divided the party into three groups, each with a teacher, and wandered off in different directions. There were three ornithologists on the island, spending a week studying the bird life, and some lighthouse keepers. We took our lunch sitting in a lee bay close to a score of nests. You had to pick your piece of grass rock to sit on, so close were the nests. Herring gulls swooped over us, uttering that strange call that caught the attention of Lawrence of Arabia when he was on holiday at Collieston on the Aberdeenshire coast a hundred miles north of May. In a letter he said, 'I wish you could hear . . . the sharpness and loneliness of the gulls questing through the spume. . . . They have the saddest, most cold, disembodied voices in the world.'

Eider ducks bobbed up and down with the swelling water in the creek, and puffins flew busily over the island with that constantly vibrating movement which one of the teachers said was like an insect movement. The lighthousemen took us to the top of the spotless lighthouse stairway, and told us about the old lighthouse at the southern tip of the island, the first in Scotland and lit by coal. We gathered some of the flowers growing richly over the island, sea campions and sea pinks, and slowly strolled back to the *Mona Lisa*. It was then that we first heard about what had been happening.

An ornithologist was waiting beside the boat. He explained with anger but nevertheless courteously that he had found five boys pelting one another with eggs. About a hundred had been destroyed and the damp white embryos littered the rocks.

It was when we got home that the full story emerged. I give the arguments back and forth in full because here we were presented (in manageable form because we didn't have much of the extra trouble that devours hours and sometimes days in establishing the facts) with the kind of problem, and the demands on any wisdom we possessed, which increasingly in the next few years teachers are going to be presented with. Those teachers, that is, who have any disposition to disentangle the matted web of motives that confuse our pupils, and to make some effort to help pupils to understand themselves and to avoid the blind and indiscriminate lashing out which hurts and wounds their pals and themselves, and makes their parents distraught.

First the pelting of one another with herring gulls' eggs. Most of the pupils who had been on the Isle of May trip had both a genuine care for bird life and an awareness that the destruction of it would terminate the facilities the Nature Conservancy had granted us to visit May and Rhum and other places. The school had a good record of respecting nature reserves. At Sandaig in Wester Ross they had picked their feet carefully between the hundreds of terns' nests. We had worked for the Nature Conservancy in building a path to a Fife hide. We had visited a piece of new land built up by sand accretion on the coast, and studied the natural growths that had colonized it, and uprooted the only 'non-natural' plants which had appeared there – fir seedlings which owed their origin to a neighbouring Forestry Commission wood. We had thought that our pupils had had so much experience of living in the countryside, mountain and glen and seashore that they would all have caught the restraint and sympathy that follows a knowledge and experience of country life. It hadn't occurred to us that close supervision would be necessary throughout the two or three hours we spent on May Isle.

One of the boys who threw eggs had been on the trip to the Isle of Rhum and had a good record. He told me, 'Before we went to May we had a talk on the bird life there. Mr Carter said that the island was over-populated with gulls and it wouldn't matter if we took some gulls' eggs.'

I admitted that this was true but that there was a difference between taking some gulls' eggs and an indiscriminate use of them as if it were a snowball fight.

He said, 'Oh aye. But it eases your mind to feel that the number of herring gulls needs to be reduced.'

'It eases your mind.' At any rate one pupil seemed uncomfortable about the incident. Some of them were taking a calm, dispassionate view of the whole affair that made us wonder if we were getting the whole business out of proportion. The skipper of the *Mona Lisa* had smiled and said, 'Boys will be boys.' But even he wondered if that summer fewer schoolboys would be permitted to sail to the island and his trade would be reduced.

We tried to reach out to the motives behind the destruction. In a country village it is difficult enough to find a bird's nest and eggs; in the Coal Town it is an event. On the May Isle here was God's plenty, eggs everywhere in carelessly scraped nests. Was it like letting a wartime child into a chocolate factory or the lean Vandals into the luxury of Imperial Rome?

Another boy had fired a catapult at an eider duck sitting on its nest. Eider ducks remain on their nests and are difficult to frighten off, and the boy said that he thought it was dead. Then he discovered that it wasn't dead but was now injured, and he decided to kill it. He dropped a large stone on it, and it struggled. He took his catapult by the rubber and hit the duck with the metal part, and still it lived. Then he tried to find a ledge of rock to put it out of sight.

I wrote a letter of apology to the Nature Conservancy, explaining what had happened, and the director generously replied that he would not in any way curtail the privileges which had previously been granted to the school. And here we come to the crux of the problem. Seven boys were concerned in these incidents. I told them that until further notice they would not go on any school trips. Two boys were taken off a week's fishing trip which was going to Rannoch and were heartbroken. I find it difficult to decide about the wisdom of these (or indeed of most) punishments. The school itself was under pressure. A newspaper rang up and said it had received an anonymous phone call from a man in Glenrothes saying that the pupils had broken five hundred eggs in the May Isle sanctuary; the newspaper published the story at length and so did two other dailies. But I noticed with interest that the local weekly newspaper, although they had sent their correspondent to interview me, forebore to publish the story. It was not the first time that I've noticed the local paper show qualities of understanding and fair play and indeed compassion lacking in the ruthless dailies. Some people were calling for retribution. It is time that we got away from the 'realists' versus 'idealists' match, which accompanies discussions on situations like this, and got down to some solid inquiry into which action is more likely to prevent a recurrence of the incidents. We generally find that children responsible for this kind of behaviour come from disturbed homes; often both parents are working, often the parents don't get on together, the child is neglected sometimes, even physically, socks and shirts unwashed, cuts and bruises untended. So they lash out at an eider duck sitting on a nest. Is it as simple as that? I don't know. But if it is, then it is nonsense in any way to punish a child for such actions. Our anger does not become us.   Although I am not a Christian I come more and more to believe that the New Testament has the rights of it, and that when we are dealing with disturbed children we should turn the other cheek and forgive until seventy times seven. And not with any feeling of being virtuous, or of martyrdom, or of masochism, but as a matter of scientific sense. We should have let the boys go fishing.

Why didn't we? Because we were frightened of the community. The community wants to see it taken out of the boys. An example must be made . . . . And in this demanding to hurt the boys, is not the community trying to find an outlet for its own frustrations; in fact doing the same to the boys as the boy did to the eider duck?

If we had not punished them, there might have been more anonymous phone calls to the newspaper, pointing out that nothing had been done to check the spread of delinquency. We in the school were already keenly aware of the vehemence of feeling directed against us, the eagerness with which our pupils' misdeeds were seized upon and published. So we punished them, and, in so doing, delayed the cure.

The Nature Conservancy emerged with credit from the situation. The Director said that since they wanted children to become responsible in their attitude to natural life they had to take risks. You don't make people responsible unless you provide situations which demand the exercise of responsibility. Once again, it seemed to me, people outside education had shown an understanding often lacking in the professional educationists.

One headmaster who lived in a Scottish industrial region told me, 'There's going to be trouble when the extra year comes. Either they'll have to get a building in the Highlands for the pupils, or else they'll have to build maternity homes. I feel as if I were sitting on top of a powder magazine.'

About this time also there was a report on the increase in venereal disease among teenagers.

I asked the Department to help us, pointing out that the work we were doing was research into how the extra year should be occupied. But the Department wouldn't listen. They replied, 'The kind of provision envisaged at Inverlair is warmly commended by the Department. In our view, however, the Inverlair project is essentially one of curricular development rather than of educational research,' and therefore it didn't qualify for a grant of money.

I tried to put myself in the position of a senior official of the Department. Would it be fair to say that his classical education shone through his letter, his skill in the manipulation of words, and irresponsibility due to his unawareness of the significance of the words he used? Is this official indifference due to the insulation which this type of education gives from ordinary living, a mental indifference reinforced by official inaccessibility? Although only fifteen miles away from the Coal Town across the Forth, they were separated by a whole education from an understanding of our pupils.

An educationist in Nottingham gave me another clue to the rejection of our appeal for funds. 'It's not regarded as research unless you've statistics,' he said.

Some light on all this lethargy, this incapacity for action, was thrown by Barbara Wootton. 'Thanks perhaps to Socrates on the one hand and to the broadcasting authorities on the other,' she wrote, 'progress in the application of scientific method to social questions still proceeds at only a modest pace.' She explained her statement. The Socratic method is negative; its object is not so much to find the answers to questions as to detect the weak points in all possible answers. BBC discussions foster this tradition; the contestants are competing in a knockout competition and there is little likelihood that a participant will modify his views on consequence of what the others say so that they can come nearer an agreed tentative solution. And Barbara Wootton pointed out that a high proportion of BBC producers were Arts graduates of Oxford and Cambridge, which means that they are Socratic traditionalists.

In teaching pupils we were constantly having to make decisions, aware that whichever decision we took, we laid ourselves open to criticism. In public life you can usually find cogent reasons for not doing anything. Perhaps we are only now experiencing the full effects of the academic education. The Socratic birds are coming home to roost.

Perhaps it was something in the climate of a Scottish education that gives us the feeling that thinkers, philosophers, writers, artists, professors are a dedicated race, objective, above the ordinary motives of mankind, commenting fearlessly on human antics and owing allegiance only in the inner light. The indoctrination is heightened by the text-books which give the impression of super-human people, actuated by noble motives above the compass of ordinary folk, who move with dignity and legislate impeccably for the good of 'the state'. They stride down the page of history with the dignity of the Roman Consul in De Quincey's opium dream.

Initially almost all the money for outdoor activities had to be raised in the school. The pupils sold cake and candy and ran raffles and dances to buy camping and climbing equipment. The school built its own canoes and sailing dinghies; twenty of them. Then gradually the local authority began to help. We could requisition ice-axes in the same way as we could requisition footballs. Then camping equipment was available, although when we asked for six primus stoves we discovered that this item was not included in 'camping equipment'. Later it was included. We were able to send more and more pupils away from the Coal Town for a week or ten days, or even for a weekend, into the countryside. Even two days made a difference to them. On a short week-end a child may have the luck to watch a dragonfly emerge from its pupa in Lochaber or listen to the fluting notes of the golden plover on the high ground above Rannoch, and store the memory against the dark days.

But we want more than these tantalizing glimpses of a different world; we want to give pupils the chance of a deeper immersion in a different way of life, and longer-enduring memories. There will be no compulsion, no pressure, no 'hurry up', no examinations. Nobody will be talked into anything. If they want to climb or ski we'll help them acquire the skills.

If they want to identify alpine plants or birds, we'll see that the knowledge is available. And when they have no yearning for activity or thirst for knowledge but just want to sit, like the Highlanders who were here before them, and watch the cloud scudding over Creag Dhubh or listen to raindrops falling through the branches after the rain has stopped, that also is an important part of growth. It is in such times that the half-submerged fears, ideas, hopes, questions, float to the surface. Already in the Coal Town school an understanding teacher has been providing for his pupils the freedom and the relaxed atmosphere where dreams and fantasies, like young children half frightened, half inquisitive, begin to venture from the shadows back into the circle of light;

and in this gathering confidence (yet still frightened) the pupils have written down some of the things that swirl through their consciousness.

FRIGHT

Now and now
the moonbeams flitter
up and down, on to my face
I am chalk white
A shadow creeps in
Now! the dark is eerie
the dark is . . . eerie

A small book of their poetry was printed. Its subjects were: Vietnam, and a monk burned in petrol, fear, the bomb, suicide, pain, the downfall of a pop star, Cerberus, the moon, God, lynchings in America. In the peace and quiet of Inverlair I think that some pupils will find release, a feeling of timelessness, a security. Perhaps this is the most important opportunity we can provide for them, the opportunity for idleness. We watched the Inverlair project being battered about like a shuttlecock from one committee to another.

The Convener of the Education Committee asked his committee finally to support or turn down the Inverlair proposal, and after prolonged and sometimes bitter discussion the committee decided to give its support by twenty one votes to nineteen. We breathed a sigh of relief and felt that at long last the way was clear for us to go ahead. But the financial implications of the proposal were discussed by the County Council; they weren't very sure about it and remitted the scheme for financial reconsideration by the Schools sub-committee. In the long game of Snakes and Ladders we had gone down a long snake and were back again at the beginning.

The Parents' Association raised money for the school, its committee giving up much free time to organize whist drives and cook for tea parties and other social functions. The Town Council gave its full support to Inverlair and allowed us to quote them as patrons of the scheme on the notepaper on which we were to issue an appeal. The Forestry Commission continued to help us every time we made a request to them. British Aluminium sent a gentle reminder suggesting that it was two years since they had offered us Inverlair as a gift. We begged for further time, hoping that the final support from the County Council was just round the corner. The Trustees of Inverlair continued to give up time for meeting after meeting, patiently to find a way round each new obstruction that the County Council put in their way, to plan for the future, to deal with legal difficulties and to find ways of raising money. Employees of the National Coal Board were particularly helpful. Several of them gave up much of their leisure to draw plans for a phased renovation, to advise on costs, to help over legal hurdles. (Some of these officials travelled long distances to attend these evening meetings.) It is the generosity of outside bodies on whom we had no claim that stays in my memory as the outstanding fact in the whole of this venture.

Over these years many pupils became good naturalists. They recognized the rich smell of birch trees and of bog myrtle. There were different shades of red in the spring, the reds of alder, birch and elm. They picked up a skull and identified it as a badger's and knew that the small leg bone lying in peat was the bone of a hare and not of a pheasant. Having identified their first wheatear they discovered that there were hundreds of them and they laughed at the derivation of the word, 'white arse'. Having identified a spotted orchis, they went on to the success of finding more un-usual orchises. They discovered that although the book was generally right in its description of a flower, there were times when the flower was not exactly as the book forecast, and in this way (I think) they were less overawed by books and began to like them more.

Parents came to the school, less critical now, to say how grateful they were for the difference that even a week in the hills had made to their children. 'He's more contented-like. He's full of beans and he's saving up to go back. He knew I was coming to see you and he told me to ask you, "When can I go back?"'

Pupils who had been out on an expedition returned at once more relaxed and more energetic. 'They return with a sort of glow on them,' Newsom wrote in his report. A member of the Coal Town staff said, 'They've got a sparkle.'

And, at intervals in this work, teachers would discuss further ideas to put into practice at Inverlair. We could ourselves instal a new septic tank if required and teach the pupils how to adapt a water-heating system to our plans for the house. We would keep ponies and bees and get the reeds out of the grass tennis court. We would learn to play the Highland game of shinty. There would be forestry in co-operation with British Aluminium's foresters who were prepared to work with us. We would ask the crofters' co-operation at Roy Bridge, four miles away, if we could come in with them in their experiments in soil reclamation.

Near the lodge there is a natural bowl-shaped amphitheatre where a whisper down at the base can be heard on the rim and we toyed with the idea of producing plays there in the summer holidays, advertising them in Fort William, perhaps persuading MacBraynes to send visitors the eighteen miles to Inverlair in buses, and putting the profits into the establishment of a pupils' theatre. We even thought we might provide the theatre-goers with tea or coffee and omelettes (from our own eggs) at two shillings a time, before they went back to Fort William. Dreams. Dreams.

We'd establish a chain of bothies throughout the west half of Scotland, so that our pupils on treks to the distant north would never be more than one day's march from a bothy and would thus be able to travel light, without tents. Inverlair would be the base camp from which the expeditions set out. Not only on foot. The technical teachers had shown our pupils how to make skis and we were eager to use them not only like the Swiss to go down mountains like an express train, but like the Swedes as a normal method of making winter journeys. We would set up weather stations, both west and east of Nevis, and prepare our own weather forecasts.

Kingsley Amis had written about 'the sullen glare in the eyes of youth'; we thought that we might try to do something about that sullen glare and we believed we could. The welfare state had produced the fittest generation of Scottish children who had ever lived and then unaccountably had ceased from its labours. It might after all be only a dream, but we decided to encourage the dreamers.

In this we were strongly supported by the Inverlair Trustees. In the midst of opposition and criticism from both political parties, it was a refreshing experience to attend one of their meetings and listen to them quietly discussing the number of spades and the cost at current prices of the cement that would be required to change a dream into a reality. Soberly they insisted that they were practical men, dealing with money and blueprints and contracts and the wording of a local government law, and dealing also with County Councils. Time and time again they counselled delay and patience and moderation, seeking to establish goodwill with the Council's members. And sometimes when I felt impatient with their advice, I remembered that for them this was a labour of love. Not one of them had a child at the school. They were busy people who could have pleaded that they needed their evenings at the fireside. They had varied backgrounds and political outlooks. I hadn't realized before how easy and simple it is to outline a proposal, and how much understanding and imagination and goodwill and knowledge and experience (quite apart from the practical work) are needed to make it a reality. The balance of imagination, as between teachers suggesting educational improvements and practical men trying to bring them about, was different from what I had thought. No ladder between earth and heaven can be built unless builders like these give it their enthusiasm. The Inverlair Trustees would have been embarrassed if I had expressed it like that to them. The way they put it was that if you believed a plan was good, it was only a matter of careful drawing and costing and preparing to convert it into reality.

Briefly their programme was this. The County Council refused to let us use Inverlair Lodge until it had been brought into a condition which would meet the minimum requirements of the Scottish Education Department. Therefore we would raise money to employ tradesmen to bring the building into this condition. This was Phase One. They drew detailed plans, met the Inverness-shire local authorities and persuaded Fife Education Committee, the Carnegie UK Trust and a local educational trust between them to contribute £2500 to meet the cost. Then they sat back to await the agreement of the County Council to the whole project.

Meanwhile we used the bus to transport small groups of pupils regularly on trips to the mountains. As we couldn't use the lodge we used tents. I joined one of the trips.

The school bus dropped us, seven boys and two teachers, at

Achallader on the south-west corner of the Moor of Rannoch, beside a farm, and a ruined castle where the Campbells started out from on a midwinter day in 1692 when they went to massacre the Macdonalds in Glencoe. This was mid-March, the end of the winter. Above the snow line at 2500 feet the snow sparkled brightly in the sun, and in the low ground there was a great brightness of water.

Hamish Brown and I had a secondary interest in this trip. The BBC had promised to consider sympathetically the draft-script for sound broadcasting which we said we'd write about the journey, and the money (£40 or more) would finance further trips for larger numbers of Coal Town pupils in the summer term. I was listening for the sounds which would make the programme real for listeners throughout Britain. The farmer and his dog were gathering the sheep across the valley. There was a sound as of a distant waterfall, but it was made by an underground stream near us. There was the squelch-squelch of boots on the boggy ground. A dixie and a bottle of milk, suspended from a pupil's rucksack, clattered together all the time, but he said it didn't worry him.

It was a beautiful afternoon. The sunshine and the heavy packs made everbody warm. We were following the drove road, clearly marked in the Ordnance Survey map, by which the drovers took their cattle from Argyll to Moray at the end of the autumn and back to Argyll at the beginning of summer, a narrow track the width of a cart, worn at the sides and green in the middle. When we stopped for our first rest, and listened to the larks and the gentle trickle of the peaty burn, we felt we were lapped in spring. A thin crust of ice on the pools showed, though, that winter hadn't quite released his grip of the valley.

A railwayman at the lonely halt of Gorton told us that he spent his spare time reading and writing. And watching television, somebody suggested. No, he said, no television. His house had no electricity. We pointed to the pylons marching past his back door but he shook his head. British Railways had not brought electricity into his house.

We set up our tents near the railway. Some of the pupils built a fire in an empty house and slept there. It was a very cold night. They were wakened at six-thirty, and before nine we shouldered our rucksacks again. The sun was shining brightly and the air was mild and spring-like in spite of the ice on the pools in the marsh. Larks were shouting away happily. The King's Cross to Fort William train passed, and, when the sound faded, the trickle of the burn came up again.

The pupils straggled out. It was a fine morning to get life and education into perspective. There were plenty of people on the Education Committee who said we were wasting our time, that it is no part of a school's job to take pupils for a picnic in the hills. But there were other people, more reasonable, who said, 'You say that it is a waste of time and life to make pupils learn about Clive and India. But what do you think you are aiming at, when you make pupils trek across the Moor of Rannoch?' I had replied that I wanted the pupils to know their own country at first hand and to know something about its past, to imagine what the whole of Scotland looked like at the end of the Ice Age when the boulders dropped out of the melting glaciers and stayed put, to work out whether one day the Moor of Rannoch could be made as fertile by sheer human effort as a similar land, Aberdeenshire, had been made.

A few miles along the way we saw a notice which said, 'Soldiers' Trenches 1745'. They were obviously drainage trenches. Sphagnum moss grew in the soggy watercourses, and on the hard, drained areas on either side grew short-stemmed heather. You could have played football on the drained ground. The trenches had been dug to empty the collected water into the Abhainn Duibhe burn that crosses the Moor. There had been a huge amount of digging, because after two hundred winters and summers of geological change their pattern was still clear. I tried to piece the story together. What wise administrator among the Hanoverians had suggested that instead of having all the Redcoats employed on guard duties at chosen posts and on patrol duties over drove tracks, to trace down Jacobites who had hidden their guns or were wearing the forbidden tartans, some of the Redcoats should be armed with spades to drain a great expanse of the Moor and suggest to the offspring of generations of cattle rustlers and freebooters that they might get a better life out of agriculture? And why had it failed? And was it still practicable? (The report of the Soil Reclamation Society, 1962, suggested that it was, the more especially since now three men with a bulldozer could achieve more in a week than a troop of Redcoats could have done in a year).

But the critics of our work in the Coal Town school were not convinced. 'What's the difference,' they asked (reasonably enough), 'between teachers who say that Fife pupils should know about the constitutional issues raised by the Jacobites rebellions, and teachers who say they should know about land reclamation schemes in the Moor of Rannoch initiated in the reign of William III?' I replied that a constitutional issue was too abstract to hold a pupil's attention, but that boys and girls, in spite of all that was said about their love of destruction, really liked to make and construct and help, and could readily understand drainage trenches and would even enjoy digging them themselves and seeing the results in the growing crops that their digging would make possible. This was one of the reasons for occupying Inverlair – the opportunity offered to enlist the pupils as active and energetic participators in the work of bringing agriculture and life back to a sour country.

I think the pupils who are uninterested in Clive and India, as remote from their lives as Ali Baba and the Forty Thieves, would like to draw up their chairs to the peat fire after a hard day in land-reclamation, and listen to the story of James Small. In 1767, at a time when the history books are full of romantic goings-on in India and Canada, Small invented the swing plough. It needed two horses and one driver; the plough it replaced needed twelve oxen and two drivers. It helped to create the agricultural Revolution and change the face of the country. From there we'd go on to the story of James Smith, a Perthshire man who ran a cotton works and found time to invent an aptly-named deep 'mole-plough' which, together with a new system of drains at fifteen foot intervals, emptied Scotland of the water that had sogged her land since the end of the last Ice Age.

But it is almost impossible to get this across to a County Council's Finance Committee. They are all for the established order, the examination system, 1066 and all that. They refuse to consider that the abolition of examinations would give a stimulus to the teaching of a subject like history. When the teacher has leisure to dwell on the ordinary every-day details and to forget the examiners' preoccupation with historical movements in which people are lifeless actors, pupils will see how like to their own lives were the lives of their forebears. We would take out pupils to the Roman camps at Trimontium (near Melrose), Ardoch (near Braco) and Inchtuthill (on the Tay). While they prepared their evening meal in a tent we'd tell them about the black Roman camps, and their cooking pots and where the Roman salt came from and what they ate. Like them the Romans had to have an eye for a camping site so that the door was away from the wind and so that rainwater wouldn't channel into it. Like them the Romans would be so much out-of-doors that they would be alert for signs of bad weather, since it made much difference to them. Like them the Romans would be up to all the dodges for keeping hot drinks from spilling in a tent, balancing the cup in a sandal perhaps, and they would have learned as our pupils did from experience not to try and keep a vessel with a hot drink warm by wrapping a garment round it because sooner or later they lift up the garment to put it on in the chill of the evening and spill out the hot drink. Did they have to cut their own tent pegs or were they issued by the quarter-master? And did some good smith make superior quality metal pegs? What did the slingers from the Balearic Islands think of being posted to Caledonia? What did they talk and sing about round the camp fire in the gloaming? At Trimontium, did a centurion talk of his father who had been in Palestine at the time of the Crucifixion? Would the diggers at Ardoch, weary after another day's work, wonder if their ditches would still be clearly seen after nineteen hundred years, and would they sit and look at the same sights as are there today – the beer-coloured river enclosing the camp on two sides, bluebells, curlews, grouse, sycamore trees?

Beyond Rannoch Station we squelched through more bogland and came on the path which is called 'The Road to the Isles' and followed it as it sloped across the flank of a long hill. At a high point we rested on a big rock and surveyed the wide landscape.

The pupils sprawled about, some of them not having taken off their rucksacks, but lying where they sank, to rest. 'It's braw,' I heard one of them say to another. I looked up from the map and asked, 'What's braw?' 'That wee cloud over there,' he said. I followed the direction. In the grey cloud there was a luminously white patch. That was all. A Coal Town pupil, resting on a high stretch of the Road to the Isles, was finding pleasure in the shape and lighting of the clouds.

While we rested, we ate handfuls of raisins, nuts and chocolate and spoke about our forebears who drove their cattle to Falkirk and Smithfield and returned over this track, talking about Lowlanders and English, highwaymen and the honest cattle-dealers they met, the dangers of the plains and the feeling of security in the hills. Like us, they drank water from the burn, but their food was handfuls of oatmeal. 'They were sturdy people,' I told my pupils, 'but not so strong nor so big and heavy as you. They didn't have the good food you have. Their mothers didn't have the ante-natal care; as children they didn't have orange juice, nor school meals!'

It was inviting to sit on the rock and to reconstruct the past because there wasn't much reconstructing to do. Like us, those drovers would be thinking of the people at home and would look forward to telling them of their journey. The clouds of March, the subdued roar of burns on the mountain slope and the sparkle of loch and river down on the Moor, the enveloping stillness – these things hadn't changed. We looked for the few changes that we could see. We had better boots than our forebears had; we had comfortable rucksacks and tents and camping equipment, we had condensed milk, and cheese from Holland, and packets of dried soup, and peaches from South Africa, and Swedish primus stoves and matches and Indian tea. We had detailed Ordnance Survey maps; they relied on landmarks. Far away and below us a diesel train slowly crossed the Moor and it looked like a darker streak of heather. In the morning we had seen a goods train taking alumina to the aluminium works at Fort William, and fertilizer for Highland crofts.

Farther west as the sun was setting over in the direction of Nevis, we lost the path when it disappeared under a snow-cap and we couldn't find it where it emerged on the other side. A sleet shower came on, darkening the landscape, and we were back squelching in bog and searching for brown tussocks to find better footing. We stayed in a tight group and kept going north because we knew that we were sure to hit Loch Ossian, which has a road all round it. The pupils were weary and footsore and hungry, and it is always depressing to see the light dwindle from the west before you know where you are going to sleep. We came to a gate in a deer fence and found that the lost path came to this gate also. The path brought us within the welcome sight of the loch. At the end of the loch we lit our candles and started up the primus stoves in a disused bothy. The glass was out of the windows and the wind came through the holes in the door. Cold and wet and miserably uncomfortable we sat on the floor and supped our soup, balancing the dixies uncertainly. One pupil spilt his soup. 'Never mind,' he said. 'I'll just put on my sausages.' There was not a word of complaint. Then by torchlight we set up our tents on short grass and crawled into our sleeping bags.

Hamish Brown went round the tents and outlined the plans for the next day's march to Kinlochleven, the distance, the terrain and its difficulty, what to look out for. After this briefing some of the pupils lay and talked and then fell asleep.

Next day the world was flooded with light and the hard, shining snow on the mountains glowed with a pink shade. The birds were singing a spring song. I heated the remains of the soup for the pupils, when they made their appearance, and cooked bacon and eggs. Gradually there leaked into the morning the warmth that you would have expected such brightness of light would have held all the time, and we all took the road again. Right ahead of us the snows sparkled on the Nevis range. The discomforts of the previous evening were a small price to pay for the elation of taking the Road to the Isles on a glorious spring morning.

I think that almost unconsciously the pupils were learning a lesson you can't learn in a classroom, that in a Highland journey, or in the journey of life, the discomforts, the depression, the wet clothes, the spilt soup and the cold, are indissolubly bound up with the top of the morning happiness. You can't have one without the other. If you are out for comfort at any price, you pay the price of missing many of the highlights. Your journey has an unmemorable dullness.

At Corrour, the Road to the Isles crosses the railway. We saw deer footprints in the soft, black, peaty earth round the skeletons of ancient trees again. A quiet south-east wind flowing through a clump of growing trees made a peaceful, unhurried kind of rhythm. We stopped at a burn and washed, and brushed our teeth. There we parted, they to continue their trek, I to return to Corrour Station and take the train back to Bridge of Orchy, pick up the school bus and take it back to the Coal Town. 'I'll be thinking of you when I'm having my coffee in the restaurant car of the train,' I told them. They laughed and moved off gaily in Indian file towards Loch Treig.

On another occasion one of the teachers had the idea of crossing the Moor of Rannoch by canoe. He said he had never heard that it had been done. We took the canoes in the school trailer to a point on the Glencoe road close to Loch Ba and, helped by a following wind, paddled north-east across the loch. There's a simplicity about this countryside once you get out of sight of the cars on the Glencoe road. You can get your bearings here.

We passed an inviting little island. It was a real Arthur Ransome scene; you could imagine Swallows and Amazons landing on the island and claiming it for their base. We ourselves landed on a little sheltered bay and looked around and set course again, sometimes glancing at the formidable mountains behind, sometimes listening to the sound of reeds rustling against the boats as we crossed through them.

A burn called the Abhainn Ba connects Loch Ba to Loch Laidon. It had been a dry winter and the rocks on the side of the burn showed that the water was six or seven inches lower than usual. Frequently we had to get out and push or pull or carry the canoe to deeper water. The pupils gaily stepped into the water up to their middles. For the last stretch of the river we did a portage. A teacher explained that it was normal for a river to drop rocks it was rolling downstream, when it met the pressure of the open loch. A fact which would be dull in a Coal Town classroom became real when it made you carry a canoe for a quarter of a mile until the loch came into view.

From there on there were five miles of Loch Laidon. The wind, although small, had backed to south-east and there was smoother water in the lee of the low hills on the right shore. Two black-throated divers sat on the water and dived in from time to time and reappeared in a new area. A smirr of rain came on. Slowly the green hills and rocky margin of the loch and little sandy beaches fell astern. We reached the end of the loch, carried the canoes over a sandy bank and into another lochan. Then wet and uncomfortable, we carried the canoes to Rannoch Station. A kindly porter agreed to get the south train to stop at Bridge of Orchy to let us get our canoes back to our camping ground. Still wet and uncomfortable and colder, we stood in the luggage van beside the canoes.

Back in the tents we made a meal, stung unmercifully by midges. I washed up, changed out of my wet clothes and crept into my sleeping bag, closing the flap of my tent. But the midges were inside the sleeping bag, busily stinging.

We continued to send parties of pupils to the cottage at Rannoch. One group of girls of twelve or thirteen years of age were very sophisticated. In school some of them were troubled and sulky, and often complained. They arrived at Rannoch wearing nylons and make-up. Even after two days, said the young woman teacher who had volunteered to be in charge of the party, a change had appeared. One of the girls discovered that she could climb trees easily. They got wet and sat in the sun until they were dry. They splashed in the water and waded through the bracken and forgot about nylons and make-up and cigarettes. They forgot the time of day. One girl asked the teacher which day it was. A hitherto timid girl was challenged to jump the burn and did it. They would sit and listen to a willow-warbler for half an hour at a time, and they lay on the grass, resting their chins on the palms of their hands while they watched endlessly the movements of a green looping caterpillar. Another girl, who had given much trouble in school, spent most of her time playing in the burn. Later I asked her, 'Did you enjoy your ten days at Rannoch?'

She laughed and said, 'Oh, yes.'

I asked her, 'What did you enjoy most?'

She replied, 'Playing in the burn.'

They had become children again.

The Education Committee agreed to make the school a grant to pay the salaries of extra staff employed at Inverlair and to subsidize part of the cost of the bed and board of thirty pupils for a month at a time, over an experimental period of two years, after which they would review the whole matter.

The venture was about to take off. We looked back over the long haul, and forward with lively expectation. A county councillor who had been in the struggle from the beginning said that at last the way was clear.

But he was wrong. Unexpectedly the County Council reversed the Education Committee's decision. They said the building was old and would take too much money to renovate and was too remote. They were in favour of the scheme in principle, but not at Inverlair. If a Beeching railway station or a closed-down village school nearer the Coal Town could be found, we should be given that as an outdoor centre. The Trustees had no opportunity to explain again that the building was sound; that it was a mile from a main road, a mile from a railway station, seventeen miles from a hospital; that a site nearer home would present the difficulty of daily transport to the hills. A councillor told me, 'And besides, Inverlair would be inaccessible because of snow for three months of the year.' I phoned the Weather Centre in Glasgow and they gave me figures for snowfall for the past ten years in Lochaber. Except for four days in one severe winter, the roads had been continually open; and even on those four days, it is possible that the snow plough had been getting through. But there was no opportunity of getting these facts to influence the County Council. The Carnegie Trust wrote courteously and said they had cancelled the grant. No money could be offered for an undertaking which had not been given 'a clear and final decision' by the County Council.

True to their promise, the County Council looked for other buildings. One was in the village of Kinloch Rannoch, but, although we would have accepted it if none other was available, we pointed out that to supervise (say) thirty girls living in a village on a main tourist highway would impose too much strain on the staff, and deny them much of the scope for experimental education that Inverlair offered. A site was proposed at Lochgoilhead. I discussed it with two eminent mountaineers and they were against it for these reasons – it held neither the geological nor the mountaineering interest of the Inverlair region, we wouldn't be able to ski there, and it was so popular with tourists that we wouldn't have the peace and quiet that the work demanded. They said that Inverlair was incomparably the best site for all the work we had in mind and suggested a fresh approach to the County Council.

I asked a councillor about it but he wasn't hopeful. Inverlair, he said, was finished.

Chapter Six
The Belt

Neither theoretical education nor theoretical Christianity seems to be tied to practice, nor is expected to be. It is strange, this curtain between the theory and the practice, whereas the common-sense of the matter suggests that they should be closely and continually related – like the plan for a bridge, and the bridge itself. Education is in a state similar to engineering two centuries ago. When the Scottish engineer, Rennie, made the Albion Mills in London, about 1788, there was no training and no precedents for engineers. They had to face a new situation on their own. This threw them upon their resources, said Smiles. They had a habitual encounter with difficulties and were compelled to be inventive.

The educational system reacts more slowly to the demands of change than do other spheres of activity. For centuries the use of corporal punishment has masked the inadequacy of the teaching and of the curriculum. How should we teachers deal with this situation? Should we alter the curriculum and hope that the need for corporal punishment will disappear? Or should we abolish corporal punishment and hope that the resulting crises will enforce an alteration in the curriculum?

In the Coal Town School we discovered that we could abolish the use of the belt on girls. I remembered reading that a teacher had been sued by parents because it was alleged that belting a girl had upset her menstrual periods. Partly to avoid being involved in a dispute of that kind and partly because of a distaste for belting girls or seeing them belted, I suggested that we could do without this punishment. There was some dissension. Teachers said, and with reason, that some girls were insolent, even foul-mouthed, truculent and difficult to handle in numbers. There was much discussion and finally, although we have not evolved a complete answer to these difficulties even yet, it became the practice that girls were not punished with the strap.

I had thought that gradually, as relationships between staff and pupils improved, as pupils understood that teachers were there as their friends to help them, and as the classroom work became more interesting and more relevant to the pupils' lives and interests, as tensions decreased, the need for the use of the belt would decrease. I had imagined that one fine day some teacher would say suddenly, 'Do you know, the belt hasn't been used in the school at all for the last six months.' It was like the hope in the Communist gospel that one day the state would wither away. After about five years I began to have my doubts about this hope. It was true that many teachers rarely used the belt; but for others this punishment remained a regular part of class routine.

It was inevitable, I suppose, in a large community staffed with independent-minded and energetic people who had hammered out of their experience clear and widely-varying outlooks on life, that dissensions would arise on how to carry out an educational revolution. Probably we were fortunate that it was only on this one question of corporal punishment that a bitter fight developed.

In trades and professions outside teaching there would be research work into such subjects as this, and the results would be available to the worker. But, generally, educational research concerns itself with recondite subjects, and we teachers have to do our own inquiry and our own experimental work and labouriously come to our own results. Sometimes we are not very sure about the validity of these, and often we get our shins bruised in the effort. I suggested that for a trial period of three months there would be no corporal punishment in the school. It was suggested that exceptions should be made. For example, there might be a case for strapping a pupil who risked his own and other people's lives and limbs by being careless with powered machinery or with scientific apparatus; and other incidents might occur to which corporal punishment would be the only effective answer. I agreed to retain the right to give corporal punishment where, as in the cases mentioned, it would be considered necessary; and that I should discuss individual incidents with the principal teachers concerned.

At the end of the three months' period, the school was involved in a major reconstruction of secondary education in the county and the introduction of the O-Grade certificate, and it was ten days after the end of the period before I called a meeting to consider the experiment. Some teachers admitted that they had gone back to the belt. The discussion in the staff meeting became a warm controversy.

Years previously a teacher told me that it was easy for me to sit in my room and drink my morning cup of tea and read the newspaper and regard the pupils in a gracious and benevolent manner, but that it was not so easy in the heat and dust of the classroom. I knew that that was true. Pupils can try you right to the limits of your patience and endurance, and beyond. I recalled with embarrassment my own classroom experience. Once, exasperated by a pupil who was inexorably truculent and obdurate, and exasperated at my own failure to deal with the situation, I got a belt and gave him six blows with it on the hand. Perhaps all teachers, except the very best, have been through this saddening and humiliating experience – humiliating because you realize that your resources for dealing with a situation like this are much less ample than you had liked to imagine. Later the figure of the pupil, valiantly taking his punishment and priding himself on his gameness, lingers in your imagination and you are angry not because he has won in the end (you grant him that) but because he has shown you up to yourself. All that noble talk on human dignity and grace in living, the indignation against those who wield the sjambok on their fellows, the impassioned appeal against the colour bar and capital punishment and all barbarity – is it just a veneer? Having caught a revealing glimpse of yourself, have you the right any more to talk against 'the ugly face of violence'?

The staff meeting to discuss corporal punishment lasted over an hour. The main points stressed were that pupils made a lot of noise in the corridors; that the fear of the belt reduced noise and bad behaviour; that pupils wouldn't respect a teacher who hadn't the use of a belt; that alternative kinds of punishment where there was delay to give time for discussion, gave a pupil more punishment through suspense than a quick blow of a belt at the time would give; that not enough money was available to schools to spend in scientific equipment to make the subject as interesting as it might be.

A teacher asked what was my objection to the belt. I said that (although the Scottish Education Department and the British Association were pleading for alterations in the content of work done in the schools) the use of the belt helped to perpetuate the old system. If we didn't use the belt we would be forced to meet the resistance of pupils by a continuous reconsideration of the nature of the curriculum. I said that the period during which we had tried to do without the belt was far too short and that it would need a period extending as far as the end of the session in the summer to try it out properly. At the end of that trial period, if a majority of the staff felt that the experiment had failed, we would resume the use of the belt. But the teachers were unanimously in favour of retaining the belt and opposed to any trial period.

I said that corporal punishment of pupils had been abolished in Norway, Denmark, Holland, Belgium, France, Austria, Italy and in most of Germany and Switzerland; but the argument carried no weight. A principal teacher, one of the best of them, a humane man who rarely used the belt, said that he felt unless he was to be allowed to keep the belt, his health would suffer. I suggested the use of the belt hadn't kept the teaching profession from being the most prone to nervous breakdowns of all the professions; I felt it was just possible that to abolish the belt would reduce tension in the classroom. Teachers gave examples of gratuitous violence committed by the pupils, and for a time the discussion hung on the nature of evil. I know clearly what they meant. A few months previously an approved school had returned a delinquent to his home; and his parents, with a word of warning sent him along to us. We sent him, later, with a group which was going for a week's mountaineering. They lived in a Youth Hostel. After they returned, the warden told me that a pile of gramophone records in the hostel common-room had been broken, and I sent for the boy.

'Was it you who broke these gramophone records, William?'
'Yes.'
'I suppose there was some horse-play going on and you rushed through the common-room and knocked them off the table and they broke. Was that it?'
'No.'
'What happened?' I asked.
William replied in a quiet voice, in which there were no traces of hostility or anger or triumph or any other emotion, 'I sat down

on a chair beside the table and broke them in ones and two over my knee.'

Thus I knew well enough what the staff meant when they talked about meaningless destruction. But I tried to suggest that it was meaningless to us only because we didn't know enough about the boy, his home background, his motives, his approved school background, to know what the meaning might be. I quoted another example.

There was a boy who had given no trouble for the first two years (between the ages of twelve and fourteen) that he had been in the school, and then in his third year reports of trouble began to come in from several teachers. It took some of the staff a long time to discover what seemed to be the reason. The boy lived with his grandmother. In order to help with the budget and also to get more spending money for himself, for the past year he had been getting up every morning, except Sunday, at 4.15 a.m. to deliver milk. In class, he was sleepy. It was, I suggested, as simple as that. I gave other examples. One teacher said, 'If you look far enough, you could find excuses for anything.' I quoted the saying 'To know all is to forgive all' but the teachers were not impressed.

Here once again we came right up against philosophy and theory. We live in two worlds. One is the real world where we are urged to be 'realists', to have practical common sense, to keep our feet on the ground and our heads out of the clouds. The other is the world of the philosophers, of the Christian teachers, idealistic, impracticable. But most people want to have it both ways; they want to have their feet on the ground and to be on the side of the angels at the same time. (Even the Nazi soldiers had 'Gott mit uns' on the buttons of their uniforms.) They make a formal bow to the educational philosophers but they feel that the work of the philosophers should be restricted to the colleges of education and the week-end educational conferences in the Highland hydros, and shouldn't overflow into the classroom.

This confusion in the classroom is a result of the confusion in men's minds about how they ought to live. They are pulled this way and that. They are capable of the most extraordinary generosity and the same people will drive the hardest and meanest of bargains just to demonstrate to others and themselves that they are not soft marks. (Several times in this corporal punishment discussion, teachers told me that pupils wouldn't respect them unless they retained a belt in the background.) The world's greatest need is to find a consistent philosophy of life. This is more important than finding a better bomb, but the bomb will be found before the philosophy because more thought is directed towards it. Thousands of distinguished people are busy, unimpeded by respect for earlier scientific outlooks, on improving the bomb. But there is no such integrated reseach for a philosophy. My own guess is that the rights of it are contained in Christianity, but the parsons are the greatest obstruction because they will go on insisting on their own interpretations of it and on every jot and tittle of their own mumbo-jumbo. If the professional scientists worked in as ramshackle and unco-ordinated a manner as the professional humanists (philosophers, professors of 'humanity', parsons, teachers) science would have advanced as little from the Renaissance as the 'humanities' have done. In the study of science, theory is the necessary complement of practice; in the study of the humanities, in teaching, for example, theory is suspect.

And although the confusion in the classroom is a result of the confusion in men's minds about how they ought to live, it is also a continuing cause of that confusion. Education, directed to the passing of examinations, is concerned with the memorizing of information. Pupils have no practice in discussing the causes of friction between one another; the lack of interest in local government; the paralysis of initiative in the face of great changes in our way of life; school government; therefore when they leave school and grow up, they have not got into the habit of regarding human problems as something which can be solved, as scientific problems can. And therefore inertia, tradition, prejudice, take the place of initiative in that field. In science, independent thought and innovation are discussed; in the humanities they are suspect.

And therefore the schools blunder on, at tremendous expense, bull-dozing over the pupils' resistance to crammed information and unintelligible disciplines, turning out angry and confused robots.

The discussion in the school became bitter. Some of the arguments for the retention of the belt carried much weight. There were, for example, uncertificated teachers in the school who were having the greatest difficulty in maintaining any kind of order, and only the threat of the belt of the principal teacher next door could help the teacher to get any work done. Again, there was a woman, graduate and certificated, enthusiastic about her work, keen to try out new methods; one of her classes, of fourteen-year-old boys, had persistently barracked her, talking with loud insolence to one another in the middle of the class, and sometimes making scarcely-concealed sexual jokes. On one occasion, when a senior teacher had had to go home because of an accident to his child, a large class had been watching a schools television programme under the supervision of a woman teacher and a newly-appointed and inexperienced man teacher. The programme was on 'Law and Order' and was illustrated by pictures of violent disorder in Trafalgar Square over the Ban-the-Bomb demonstrators and equally violent scenes at fascist meetings in London. In all these scenes the police figured largely. The pupils were angry at the violence shown by the police. When the programme finished, the pupils began to stamp their feet and make a noise and refused to stop. The woman teacher said she could have handled the situation but for the fact that I had forbidden the use of the belt. She was probably right. She came and asked me to come to the classroom. I asked the pupils who had made the row to stand. Nobody stood. I told them I took a dim view of their making a row in the absence of the senior teacher and a dimmer view of their failure to admit it. One boy stood up. Then another two. Shortly a dozen were on their feet. I sent the rest of the class away and sent for the School Council. They listened to the account of what had happened and I left them with the dozen pupils who had made the row. The Council didn't take long to make their decision. It was that the pupils should be severely belted. So I got out a belt, long disused, and belted them one each.

In the meantime the teachers had got together and sent a statement to the Director of Education saying that my refusal to allow them to use the belt had made it impossible for them to do their work, and asking for his advice. I think the statement was signed by every full-time certificated member of the staff.

Feeling sorry for myself, I went to see one of the teachers whom I knew best. I asked him how often he had belted his own son, a likeable, energetic youngster aged fifteen. He said only once. I pointed out that according to the law, a teacher is *in loco parentis* and suggested that these Latin words meant that a teacher should treat his pupils as he would treat his own son. The teacher replied that it was more difficult to run a class than to run a family. He added that his reason for signing the letter to the director was that he objected to dictatorship, the dictatorship which took from teachers the freedom to run their class in their own way. I said that if Britain joined the Common Market and European customs and usages were introduced into Britain, the belt might be abolished in Britain. What would he do if the Director of Education sent along a note one day saying that from the beginning of the following session no corporal punishment would be used in schools? Would he regard that also as dictatorship? He said that that would be different.

I realized that a complex of emotions affected this issue and made it intractable to discussion. Further argument was useless. A letter came to me from the Director of Education – 'for the attention of the staff'. I called a staff meeting and read it to them. It said that the policy on corporal punishment should be one which was willingly adopted by the whole staff. It was the Education Committee's practice to consult teachers on matters of policy, particularly where their daily work was affected, and I shouldn't impose a policy with which so many of the staff were in complete disagreement.

I added briefly, 'You've got what you wanted. From tomorrow the use of the belt will be restored. I had hoped that at the end of the session eight months from now, when the no-belting rule had had a real try-out, there would have been a vote of the whole staff on the success or failure of the experiment. For me this is a major defeat. From the time the school opened over five years ago we have been working out a policy together. It wasn't just an orthodox school which happened occasionally to send parties of pupils on expeditions to the mountains. I thought that the mountain expeditions and the opposition to the use of the belt were integral parts of the same policy, based on a new attitude to children. It hasn't worked out that way.'

Chapter Seven
The Establishment

In school the inadequacy of the natural gifts of ordinary people is stressed also by a comparison with the people in authority. A child's idealism and worship of the heroic are used for the Establishment's purpose. Not very nice people, Wat Tyler and his mob. Not noble characters, like the Black Prince for example. There was Richard II on his horse (the horse makes a lot of difference) courageously telling the rabble in London, 'I myself will be your leader.' The sequel is not stressed. Children visiting the Chapel of St John in the Tower of London are invited to visualize the scene where the mob broke in upon the prayers of the archbishop and killed him. It is only recently and gradually that I have realized the power of the accumulated details of the propaganda trick that my teachers were playing on me. I don't blame them, for they were themselves taken in by it. The majority of the population are coming of age. They want to be told the story of human life on the earth, and they are becoming impatient with the school examination questions which keep pupils' attention away from the dark corners of our political history. The facts unearthed by Cobbett, for example. I was brought up to believe that figures like Pitt were cast in the heroic mould, a cut above ordinary, erring humanity. People like Cobbett and Tom Paine were minimized and devalued in the history books. Cobbett showed that in less than a year Pitt had handed out annual pensions of £38,000, and Addington had given his twelve year old son an official job worth £3000 a year. It was at this time that Heine referred to 'the distinguished thieves who plunder England.'

The increasing emphasis on technological training means an increasing denial of the needs of the human spirit. As far as children are concerned, it means an increase in delinquency as the only available protest against this kind of exploitation and, when they become adults, it means a more feverish pursuit of trivialities that don't bring real satisfactions. If at this time of political bankruptcy, the educationists don't reconsider the whole nature of society and life on earth, and start caring for people for their own sake and helping them to find the things that belong to their peace, there is likely to be violence and turmoil. We shall have to begin at the foundation and create a society in which we acknowledge everybody as first class citizens and treat them so. Throughout history the established minorities have tried to avoid taking this way out. Now it begins to look as if it is the only way.

The experimental schools, trying out new methods, are fighting a battle on two fronts. They cannot direct all their energies into the problem of how to forge a new educational system because they have all the time to be looking over their shoulders at public opinion and the authorities. In the old days, a good school was a quiet school. Creative work and scope were of less importance than giving the authorities the comfortable feeling that everything was under control. There were neat rows of desks, each box-like classroom quiet. The principal quality looked for in teachers was that they should be 'good disciplinarians'. There was a subdued tone in the school. It is only lately that I see these traditional recommendations in the perspective of history. This was the main function of schools – keeping pupils quiet and in order. The public and their elected representatives usually take this view. In this respect most Labour councils are just as traditional as the Conservative councils; they want the new comprehensive schools to be as quiet and regimented as the grammar schools. And therefore the experiments carried out by the Coal Town staff invited the suspicion of the authorities. We could do much more if they would give us their backing.

The central education authorities are equally remote. They don't understand how serious the situation has become, nor how dramatically it may develop. We feel that we are defending a beleaguered city, but they don't see it that way.

They come to us pleading for experimental work, for a new approach to education. But they will not accept the implications of experimental work. For example, parents criticize this work for the very reason that it is new, not what they were brought up to regard as education. Therefore, for the most part, the only experimental work done is of the innocuous kind: that is to say, work that won't invite attacks by the parents. Teaching machines are all right; they are regarded as a more technical way of doing the same work as the teacher did before with chalk and blackboard. Expensive ship cruises are all right; their very expensiveness gives status to the contributing parents. Green blackboards instead of black, splinterproof gymnasium floors, richly lit stages are accepted because they have an air of progress about them.

I wish able people in the universities would get down to tackling the problem realistically, and with as much urgency as they tackle, say, metal strain in aeroplanes. I am quite sure this problem is capable of solution if the same energy and finance were brought to it. By taking thought, human beings can prevent a crash whether of an aeroplane or a democratic system.

The discouraging thing is that there are no signs of determined effort to make democracy work. There is a dispiriting lack of initiative amongst civil servants. They won't take the risk of trying something that hasn't been tried before. And since our civilization is changing much more rapidly than any other civilization did, most of the things already tried are not much good. There is a mental lethargy about these civil servants; they live in a state of elegance and Roman imperturbability. Analytically, they are very good. They can size up a situation in well chosen and unemotive words, adjudicating fairly among the parties to the situation. And, having delivered their diagnosis, they go home. Imagination, the creative ability to find new solutions, is not their strong suit. All their thinking (well, the thinking that gets through to official reports) is done within the accepted idiom of the time. I long to ask them if they accept the truth of the parable of the ninety and nine – or do they think this is starry-eyed idealism and economic folly and that Christ was talking through his hat. I wish we could dispel this philosophical fog in which civil service opinion is enshrouded. The worst thing they can do to the Christian religion in which they nominally believe is to fail to give to young people clear answers about where they stand. Do they or do they not believe in not killing, in loving your enemy, in not judging and in taking no thought for the morrow? And it's no good giving some formula: 'On the one hand . . . but on the other . . . .' Our young people have had a bellyfull of this kind of formula, and would regard the administration as the author of *Revelations* regarded the Church of the Laodiceans: 'I know thy works, that thou art neither cold nor hot: I would thou wert cold or hot. So then because thou art lukewarm, and neither cold nor hot, I will spue thee out of my mouth.'

A whole lot of consequences would follow from a remaking of education. Once start inquiring into the nature of your education and you begin to shed convictions and prejudices, the fear of creepy-crawlies, of miscegenation, a voting pattern, dependence on coal fires and bacon and egg breakfasts, the accepted religious pattern, induced feelings and attitudes. My grandfather in Banffshire, biting into a tomato for the first time and expecting it to taste like a particularly lush apple, spat it out. My father wouldn't eat the new-fangled food, lettuce, which my mother introduced to the diet, and called it 'cows' food'. The more you look into it, the more apparent does it become that the foundation of our lives is a tissue of induced beliefs. I was brought up to admire a first class honours degree, and it took me a long time to recover from the relative failure of getting a second class one. This is the whole pattern of 'keeping up with the Joneses'. Once society and your education (in the broadest sense) have filled you with admiration of whatever it is the Joneses have got that you have to keep up with – fitted carpets, a big television set, a refrigerator, a child at the grammar school, a son at Oxford, a Jaguar car, holidays in Brittany, the Dalmatian coast, or Hawaii (and like a mountain, the Joneses go on presenting another summit to scale as you perspiringly reach what you had thought was the ultimate peak) – you become engrossed in the chase, and have not time or opportunity to stop and consider if it is worth pursuing. All sorts of people from Isaiah to Matthew Arnold have wasted their breath saying this, but the establishment's educational system has been too much for them. Assuredly the establishment doesn't want people to consider whether they are spending their money for that which is not bread. The consequences would be much too upsetting.

There is a similarity in the development of emergent countries and of emergent children. Colonial governors and headmasters (both largely products of the classical tradition), although sensitive and understanding people, have counselled caution. It's a sad thought that it has taken violence and the threat of further violence to counteract the advice of the colonial governors. If it had been left to the wisdom of the governors, I suppose there isn't one African country that would be self-governing today. The children haven't such resources at their command as would compel the granting of greater freedom to them. Or hadn't, until recently. But now there loom ahead powerful reinforcements to their capacity for violence and the headmasters are beginning to take amongst themselves the same kind of counsel that was forced on the colonial governors. Nevertheless the educational conferences will go on without coming to any resolute action for change – that is the pattern that recent colonial history suggests – until violence is upon them. (And this irresolution, this dilatoriness, is itself part of an educational tradition forged during long ages of slow development; the ministries and educational departments are like the dinosaurs of the Mesozoic, unable to adapt to the new conditions of rapid change.)

In Scotland in the eighteenth century most university students were boys taking their MA degree at the age of sixteen and learning philosophy without knowing what it was about. They had to repeat Arisotle's definitions and to memorize lectures on Grotius and Puffendorf all in Latin. Their minds (said Graham in his *Social History of Scotland in the Eighteenth Century*) were crammed with terminology no dictionary could explain. This tradition of using words without much real understanding of their meaning persists in Scottish education to this day, together with a belief that the duller the education is, the more good it does to you. On festive occasions in the eighteenth century these young students performed a Latin play in which the various parts of speech were personified and appeared to argue their respective claims to precedence over the rest. One might have thought that many people would have asked wherein lay the value of this kind of education. But the majority of people, and especially the middle class, are eager to submit their children to such school-work, believing that our educational system is a noble heritage, a product of enlightenment broadening down from precedent to precedent. In so far as people think about this at all, there is a feeling at the back of their minds that everything has been wisely ordered. This is where pageantry, pomp and circumstance come in. How could we fail to be persuaded of the wisdom of those professors at a graduation ceremony in their brightly coloured medieval caps and gowns moving in procession to the music of *Gaudeamus igitur*, played by the pealing organ?

The quality most needed both by the administrators, hesitant and enslaved to habit, and the adolescents with their idealism and ferocity and sensitivity to rejection, is imagination. But this is above all a quality that the administrators lack and the system discourages. I don't think the discouragement of imagination is a historical accident, the result only of the indolence of the educationists. The Romans similarly discouraged imagination. Their strongly disciplined civilization was like a channel which directed water power in one direction and not in another. They channelled intelligence, they knew what they wanted it to do for them. It was not a free intelligence wandering like the wind where it will, seeing technical possibilities, catching sudden glimpses of relationships in unlikely places, seeing new patterns in music and art and literature, new ways of getting across to other people the things in one's own mind, new ways of persuading people to get on well together. Two centuries ago village blacksmiths, unimpeded by an education, became the inventors of the Industrial Revolution. Today we desperately need inventors for the social revolution, but most of those who might be making that contribution are hobbled by their education. In a recent book, Richard Acland said we were entering the third chapter of the story of man on the earth. The first was the hunting stage. The second began ten thousand years ago with the invention of agriculture or seven thousand years ago with writing and the keeping of records and accounts. From this civilization, at once individualistic and authoritarian, people like Wyclif, Rousseau, Washington, Bentham and Marx have in different ways encouraged us to eject ourselves. Shaftesbury, speaking on reducing the hours in the cotton industry, was asked by Peel, 'Will you legislate for all?' The answer given later was, of course, 'Yes', but it was a new idea and it took a long time for people to accept it. Ideas of this kind were regarded like strangers in a primitive society, with fear and hostility. It was a novel idea to the individualistic, authoritarian age and really belongs to the new age on which we are entering. It is the job of the teachers to construct (or rather to help to grow) a new embedding culture based on the feeling that 'ultimately every man and women is as valuable as every other, and that each is equally privileged and burdened to make the basic decisions for himself.'

This idea is so novel to the élite-based educational system in which all of us have been brought up, as to seem at first sight ridiculous. I think few people are really aware of the educational system's violent opposition to new ideas. We have been so indoctrinated with the idea that we are the liberals that it seems unthinkable to suggest that our system is obscurantist. We can't see ourselves as others see us, but if we look at other countries and see them from the outside (and compare this view with the countries' view of themselves), it should help us to get a different view of ourselves. In a Panorama interview in 1966 Mrs Gandhi, Prime Minister of India, spoke of 'giving people education in the broadest sense, making them receptive to new ideas.' We can appreciate, of course, that the Brahmins need to have their ideas sorted out (sacred cows holding up the traffic in Delhi, and all that), but that applies only to the Hindus. No sacred cows in Britain.

Christianity has been saying for some time now, but not with any conviction, that everybody is ultimately as valuable as everybody else and that each is equally privileged and burdened to make the basic decisions for himself. People were not meant to take it seriously. But the present state of the nation and particularly of the educational jungle, bellowed at us in headlines almost daily, shows that the old individualistic and authoritarian age is in decline. The self-appointed élites have had it. Negroes, for example, won't stand for them any more. The élite-based political parties in Britain – Tory, Liberal, Labour and Communist – suddenly seem to be amazingly similar to one another, and irrelevant to the sullen and angry eyes of youth. The secondary modern pupils (whether so described in the Tory schools or masked in the Labour comprehensives) are serving notice on us that they refuse to be patronized any more. That means that (however strange it may seem to our élite-indoctrinated thoughts) we shall have to start treating all human beings with the same respect. And from there it will be easier to find and tap a new emotional dynamic, to put life and purpose and community back into a society which is at odds with itself.

A quarter of a century ago this would have been a noble, nebulous, Utopian pipe dream that nobody believed would become real. Today it is different because tomorrow there will be an increase in vandalism and apparently inexplicable acts of cruelty, and in the 1970s the younger generation may be tearing the whole thing to bits.

Chapter Eight
The Verdict

The introduction of comprehensive education meant that the school in the Coal Town faced the possibility of being taken over by the traditional and orthodox grammar school. If that happened most of the experimental work would cease. Experimental work is by its nature uncertain of results and that is a risk that few, if any, grammar schools can take.

We believed in comprehensive education. We understood the intention behind the policy and had been putting it into practice. The head of the physical education department, a former first division football player, was absorbed in the training and progress of the school's first team, and proud of their success. But the welfare and well-being of *all* his pupils were of equal concern to him. The fact that some of them were slow and clumsy on the football field did not make him any the less concerned for them. He threw just as much energy into encouraging and cajoling the slow starters to train and persevere until they could measure up to the Duke of Edinburgh Award demands; run a hundred yards in thirteen seconds; swim a hundred yards in one minute and thirty seconds; make a long jump of fourteen feet and a high jump of four feet one inch.

He inveigled them into cross-country runs and five-a-side football, into learning to swim and to canoe and to dance the Eightsome Reel. The shy and the embarrassed and the awkward were persuaded from their seats at the Christmas party, and discovered to their delight that they could actually enjoy dancing the St Bernard's Waltz and the Dashing White Sergeant, almost before they had fully realized that they had left the safe anchorage of the seats round the walls and were aswim with countless other craft on the floor. He was humorously tolerant of the pupils who got stuck half across the horse in the gym, and they laughed at themselves good humouredly. There was a gaiety about it. Quips and light-hearted banter were freely exchanged between teacher and pupils, interspersed with serious discussion and advice. And the whole business was a triumph of human relationships because the pupils sensed that here was a teacher interested in their welfare, concerned for their success, without favourites, who put in extra work and extra hours (not only ungrudgingly but also as if it were a pleasure to do it) to run competitions and evening clubs and Friday evening dances on their behalf.

For me this was the essence of comprehensive education, an equal concern for all. And the pupils had such a sense of security, of not being laughed at or being held up to ridicule or being compared unfavourably, that none of them who were clumsy or awkward at PE or games had any sense of grudge towards those who were chosen for the first team and won acclamation. They didn't feel aggrieved any more than a member of a local miners' brass band, struggling with his cornet, feels aggrieved when he hears a faultless professional performance. Instead there was a genuine and generous appreciation. It is the insecure child who feels resentment and withholds praise.

This is what comprehensive education means, at any rate, to our way of thinking. It was something new in education, an attempt to educate the whole population, showing equal concern for all. The old establishment in which there were a few rich and many poor was dissolving, but a new minority were trying to maintain or re-establish the old pattern by using the schools to make a distinction between a few 'academic' and many 'non-academic'. When you try to track down this word 'academic' you find it is as insubstantial as a mirage – one of those words by which people have sought to trap and fix children in a rigid framework. We are terribly easily taken in by words; if there is a word, we believe there *must* be a thing which the word represents. Parents believe that there is a fundamental distinction between the few 'academic' and the many 'non-academic' children; otherwise (they reason) these words wouldn't exist. One of the most pressing duties laid on teachers today is to get children to understand that some words don't mean anything. They were invented not to define and reveal but to obscure, to suggest non-existent bogies, to mislead. Actually it's adults whom we have to warn against words. A child sees more clearly. A white child playing with a black child has no awareness of colour bar; this is an adult idea. The history of mankind is the story of attempts to escape from a prison of words. So deeply has the voice of our education bitten into our unconscious that people have been prepared to lay down their lives – for words.

Children are realistically aware of differences but unworried by them until their education tells them that certain differences are the great dividers. On one side of the chasm, the chosen pupils; on the other side, the rest. It is then that the sense of difference becomes obsessive, and hostility and a sense of grievance arise. That is why occasionally our rejected Coal Town children topple the grammar school children from their bicycles on the way home from their so separate schools. I believe that the Labour policy-makers genuinely wanted to heal this breach when they brought in comprehensive education. The policy is good, and indeed, inevitable. But the story of the attempt to carry out this policy shows what happens when a revolutionary new idea has to be realized by people who have had a severely traditional education. New wine and old wineskins.

In the Coal Town school we had been working, as we believed, in the spirit and intention of the comprehensive policy. All of our pupils were of equal concern to us. If sometimes we gave more attention to pupils who had unhappy home backgrounds, that was only an attempt to even things up. The distinguished example of the teacher of physical education could, we believed, be followed by all teachers. We didn't believe in 'streaming', that is, dividing up pupils according to the marks they had made in the eleven plus. But in the new comprehensive schools, the Labour local authority was determined, the pupils *would* be segregated from one another. The traditional rigid Scottish education was to continue almost completely unaffected by a revolutionary new doctrine; it indicated an admirable toughness in the establishment, a determined resistance to change and an ability to survive.

In the interests of comprehensive education the school which had been based on the spirit of the comprehensive revolution more truly than any other school in the county was to be closed, and its pupils and some of its teachers sent to the local grammar school. We saw clearly, as if it were a text-book illustration, how superficial a political change can be if it is not underpinned by a fundamental change in the educational system.

'If you are to get O-grade results,' an inspector said, 'you'll have to put more pressure on the pupils.'

At a staff meeting we discussed Patricia. She was an intelligent girl but her work had fallen back. 'We should sling her out of the O-grade class' said one of her teachers. 'In the educational jungle each school is judged on its O-grade results, and only on its O-grade results. Some of the pupils are working well. Patricia isn't. If we throw her out of the class, that will give a better chance to the pupils who *are* doing well.'

Another teacher said, 'No. We should leave her in the class. But we should put more pressure on her. Much more pressure.'

These teachers were themselves under pressure. The senior chief inspector had attacked the school for its O-grade results in English. The Director of Education and a local county councillor had been quoted publicly as having attacked these results. Parents clamoured for O-grade successes; and that was understandable, because most employers demanded them. And therefore it was reasonable that the teacher thought that we should put much more pressure on Patricia.

The woman adviser intervened. 'Patricia's father died last month. Heart trouble. Her mother left him a year ago. Patricia and two younger brothers have been living with her grandparents. The grannie is seriously ill. Isn't there enough pressure on the girl?'

We moved on to a consideration of the other candidates for the O-grade. But we all felt a dull anger at the mandarins of the Scottish Education Department and the examination juggernaut to which they gave such a single-minded devotion. And we were all the angrier because we felt that they were probably kind people, good to their own families, and that it was their own restricted upbringing which was responsible for their lack of imagination, their failure to visualize the effects of their policy upon other children. They would probably be shocked to hear it suggested that their examinations were making life almost intolerable for a considerable number of fourteen- to sixteen-year-old children. And dumb-founded if anyone should apply to them that most devastating of denunciations: 'But whoso shall offend one of these little ones . . . it were better for him that a millstone were hanged about his neck, and that he were drowned in the depth of the sea.'

Well, now, it is necessary to say that we in the Coal Town see many of 'the least of these' (having failed their exams) stumbling. Who is to blame? That is hard to say. But it is time that it was said in clear terms that those who have some power to keep their feet from stumbling are failing them, are dragging their own feet. I refer to the Education Department. We see pupils looking desperately for help and guidance while the Department publishes fine sounding memoranda and asks the pupils to prepare answers to questions like, 'What was the position of the Scottish Church in the sixteenth century?' We see our pupils full of doubt and fear and hate, but especially doubt. The tragedy of all this is that we see the infinite potential hovering just out of reach. It's like a television programme blurred and indistinct. It needn't be so. A little alteration of switches could make it loud and clear. Occasionally we get glimpses of the picture when the set is properly tuned. At the Christmas concert scores of pupils were, if I may use their phrase, 'switched on'. In the massed choir some sat upright, others leaned slightly forward in their intentness, watching the teacher who was conducting them and answering with a smile her smile of encouragement. The guitarists looked like a Goya group, feet splayed out, or legs tucked under the seat, in an attitude of complete unselfconsciousness. The plaintive recorders played a simple melody. Curiously remote behind a transparent gauze screen on the stage, shepherds and Rubens-like angels seemed to be part of the landscape, together with the painted background of cattle shed and tree and sheep and hills and night sky. It was, as people say, 'out of this world'. And at the end-of-term service there was this same sense of the infinite in music, a soaring descant suddenly releasing goodwill and energy, the high notes of the cornet at the last verse of a carol giving a sense of excellence and complete involvement.

The charm doesn't last long. The spell is broken. But it keeps returning fitfully, tantalizingly. A glint of merry mischief lights up sullen eyes. A full and generous and unasked apology redeems an ugly scene. It is as if the pupils were haunted by glimpses of an ampler life.

Thou, over whom thy Immortality
Broods like the Day, a master o'er a slave.

And similarly, fitfully, sparks of generosity light up official publications. These words come from *Health of the School Child* (HMSO, 1960):

> Children can learn, in order to make life bearable, to 'imprison their unhappiness', to set up a facade and to comply, and it is easy to describe this as being happy. The price may be an outlet in some physical reaction such as soiling, or asthma, or even more subtly, an impoverishment of the capacity for living, stifling spontaneity and hindering intellectual as well as social development.

Reading between the lines of that paragraph I can see clear signs of the 'new modes of thought and a change of heart' that Newsom pleaded for. In many schools there are teachers with quite other standards of value than those on which the Department normally puts store. It is on this leaven of teachers and administrators that our future depends.

But the odds are against them. Administrators want tidy, efficient administration. They want large-scale production, big schools, computerized examination results. They can't be bothered with small schools, concerned with the needs of individual children.

The woman adviser helps a daughter to bath a bed-ridden mother, finds warm clothing for girls who come to school in winter in thin dresses, sorts out rows at home, saves the psychiatrists much time by writing out full reports on the children referred to them, finds employment for delinquents (taking the employers fully into her confidence), brings back children who have run away from home, admonishes parents for indifference to their children. Latterly parents have begun to come to her for help with their own marital troubles, even when these have no reference to the children. Once upon a time, these parents would have gone to the parson (but they have long ceased to go to church) or to the doctor (but queues are waiting to get into his surgery on a cold winter afternoon and he hasn't the time). The school shows signs that it could fulfil a new need and become a centre for the community, fulfilling the same needs as a monastery did in the Middle Ages and helping to knit the community into one. That is what we understand by the idea of a comprehensive school. But if the pupils are to have the sense of community, of being members one of another, of belonging, it can't be a big school. In a big school the individual pupil is swamped, he feels his own littleness and he feels insignificant. Our own woman adviser has little enough leisure looking after five hundred pupils. Nevertheless she feels she might still cope if there were eight hundred pupils. But not more.

The Labour Party thought otherwise. They were all for big schools. We had believed that the comprehensive system would help our pupils and would support us in our efforts to restore to them, the sons and daughters of Fife miners, the feeling of their individual worth, the confidence to walk the earth upright, unabashed by anybody. We hadn't realized that the Labour Party accepted the old curricula, the old academic assessments on children. We didn't really believe that the comprehensive system would destroy the school. When the news came, it came as a surprise.

I asked Fife Education Committee why they proposed to close down the Coal Town school. They had a simple answer. 'The estimated secondary population in this area in 1970 is just over 3000. That's too small for three schools. We're reducing the number to two. Yours is the oldest building and will be closed.'

Other Penguin Education Specials

Children in Distress

Alec Clegg and Barbara Megson

Two out of every hundred children have to be given direct help by the State – whether it be psychiatric, social or medical.

But are these the only children 'in distress'? What about those children who do not qualify for State help?

Alec Clegg and Barbara Megson estimate that perhaps 12 per cent of our children desperately need help, but do not qualify to receive it. *Children in Distress* paints an agonizing picture of child distress, based on the authors' long experience in educational administration. They argue that it is the schools – in daily contact with the children – that are the agencies best suited to help this large and saddening section of our child population.

'... this book, containing a wealth of information and ideas based on the experience of very many schools, can help teachers who want to help their problem pupils, but just do not know how to start. It can help them, probably, more than any other single volume.'
The Times Educational Supplement

Education for Democracy

Edited by David Rubenstein and Colin Stoneman

The time for a radical manifesto on British education is long overdue. For over twenty-five years the struggle to democratize our system has been held back by those who see the proper function of education as the production of an élite and, as the most efficient means of effecting this, the labelling of children as A's or D's at the earliest possible opportunity. Those children who do not meet the requirements of the current élite have had some reason to be disconsolate about their fate.

Here at last – appropriately at a time when the 'backlash' is receiving all the attention, if not actually gaining the upper hand – is a bold definition of the nature and purpose of 'education for democracy'.

The contributors to this collection, all of whom have to grapple daily with these problems on the lecture-hall or classroom floor, do not attempt to put forward a single, easy solution. But whether they are writing about the content of the primary curriculum or university examinations, about slum schools or the new technology of learning, there is one fundamental belief which they all hold in common. They demand an education system which cares about *all* children, regardless of race, class or intelligence, and which helps to build a democratic society by upholding the qualities of compassion and respect within its own walls.

'This is a thought provoking and stimulating book which raises the question as to what education for democracy should be.'
Tribune

Neill and Summerhill
A Man and His Work

A Pictorial Study by John Walmsley

A. S. Neill is the most famous schoolmaster in the world. What he has succeeded in doing at his school, Summerhill, has been perhaps the most important single reason for our increasing respect for school children as individuals.

This remarkable collection of photographs and reminiscences is a tribute to this man and his work. We once asked John Walmsley, the photographer, why it included so few pictures of Neill himself. 'The children,' he replied, 'are pictures of Neill.'

'Walmsley's pictures and the reminiscences of a score of friendly contributors provide a refreshingly uncultish testimony to the life-work of a humane educator.'
New Society

The School That I'd Like

Edited by Edward Blishen

In all the millions of words that are written annually about education, one viewpoint is invariably absent – that of the child, the client of the school. It is difficult to think of another sphere of social activity in which the opinions of the customer are so persistently overlooked.

In December 1957 the *Observer* organized a competition for secondary school children to remedy this, and invited essays on 'The school that I'd like'. We publish a selection of the entries here. They constitute a passionate and sustained attack upon our present educational order. Their intelligence and originality are only rivalled by their unanimity. The writers demand to be allowed to think, to encounter head on the raw material of learning, to be at risk, to escape from boredom into the joy of discovery, to be *partners* in their education. No one will read this selection without feeling some shame at what we have done to these children. Who will answer them? Who will explain to them why they should not have what they demand?

'I am tired of hearing that the hope of my country lies in my generation. If you give me the same indoctrination ... how can you expect me to be any different from you?' *15-year-old girl*

'The essays are remarkably articulate. ... This is a stimulating and challenging book.'
Teaching